Praise for *I Beat the Odds*

"I'd understand if some people out there felt like another retelling of the Oher story was flogging a dead horse, but personally, I felt like there's a need for Oher's own opus. . . . Don't get me wrong—Sean and Leigh Anne Tuohy are fantastic people with their own story to tell (they're getting a book deal, too, by the way), but Michael Oher is more than the glorified prop he became in the Hollywood version of his life."
—Yahoo! Sports

"The real Michael Oher just might be the first person with more sparkle and good looks than his movie counterpart. . . . The book offers a harrowing first-person account from a child's point of view of the Dickensian conditions many American kids endure."
—USA Today

"With the release of his memoir . . . Oher finally takes ownership, filling the gaps in the familiar narrative and somehow managing to make his journey from the streets to stardom seem even more amazing and compelling. . . . *I Beat the Odds* is thoughtful and heartfelt, a young man coming to grips with an amazing journey that required the distance of years and perspective to fully grasp."
—*The Washington Post*

I BEAT THE ODDS

FROM HOMELESSNESS, TO *THE BLIND SIDE,* AND BEYOND

MICHAEL OHER

with

DON YAEGER

GOTHAM BOOKS

GOTHAM BOOKS
Published by Penguin Group (USA) Inc.
375 Hudson Street, New York, New York 10014, U.S.A.

Penguin Group (Canada), 90 Eglinton Avenue East, Suite 700, Toronto, Ontario M4P 2Y3,
Canada (a division of Pearson Penguin Canada Inc.) · Penguin Books Ltd, 80 Strand, London
WC2R 0RL, England · Penguin Ireland, 25 St Stephen's Green, Dublin 2, Ireland (a division of
Penguin Books Ltd) · Penguin Group (Australia), 250 Camberwell Road, Camberwell, Victoria
3124, Australia (a division of Pearson Australia Group Pty Ltd) · Penguin Books India Pvt Ltd,
11 Community Centre, Panchsheel Park, New Delhi–110 017, India · Penguin Group (NZ),
67 Apollo Drive, Rosedale, Auckland 0632, New Zealand (a division of Pearson New Zealand
Ltd) · Penguin Books (South Africa) (Pty) Ltd, 24 Sturdee Avenue, Rosebank, Johannesburg
2196, South Africa

Penguin Books Ltd, Registered Offices:
80 Strand, London WC2R 0RL, England

Published by Gotham Books, a member of Penguin Group (USA) Inc.

Previously published as a Gotham Books hardcover edition

First trade paperback printing, February 2012
5   7   9   10   8   6

Gotham Books and the skyscraper logo are trademarks of Penguin Group (USA) Inc.

All photos are courtesy of the author unless noted otherwise.

THE LIBRARY OF CONGRESS HAS CATALOGED THE HARDCOVER EDITION AS FOLLOWS:
Oher, Michael.
I beat the odds : from homelessness, to the blind side, and beyond /
by Michael Oher, with Don Yaeger.
p. cm.
ISBN 978-1-59240-612-8 (hardcover)   978-1-59240-638-8 (paperback)
1. Oher, Michael.   2. Football players—United States—Biography.
3. University of Mississippi—Football.   4. Baltimore Ravens (Football team)
I. Yaeger, Don.   II. Title.
GV939.O44A3   2011
796.332092—dc22
[B]   2010045531

Printed in the United States of America
Set in Fairfield LT • Designed by Elke Sigal

While the author has made every effort to provide accurate telephone numbers and Internet
addresses at the time of publication, neither the publisher nor the author assumes any responsibility for errors, or for changes that occur after publication. Further, the publisher does not have
any control over and does not assume any responsibility for author or third-party Web sites or
their content.

Penguin is committed to publishing works of quality and integrity.
In that spirit, we are proud to offer this book to our readers;
however, the story, the experiences, and the words
are the author's alone.

CONTENTS

FOREWORD

Of all the people who helped me succeed, the one who I think comes out on top is Miss Sue, my incredibly dedicated, incredibly wise, incredibly patient tutor. As I broke a sweat over the books each night during my senior year of high school, trying to make the 3.8 GPA required for college even to be an option for me, Miss Sue was there each and every step of the way. And there was no class that made me sweat harder than Ms. Henderson's English class. She had a tough class with a lot of homework—more than all my other classes put together, it seemed—and each time I earned a passing grade, Miss Sue and I would celebrate, because that really took some doing.

That being said, I am pretty sure Ms. Henderson is still in awe, not only that I wrote a 250-page book, but that I wrote a 250-page book that ended up becoming a *New York Times* bestseller. I have to admit that I'm kind of in awe myself.

When I started working on this book in the summer of 2010, I had no idea it would end up being as big as it was. I figured that my main audience would be foster parents and guardians buying it for their kids and reading it themselves. There would probably be some teachers and social workers interested in it, too, and maybe a couple of die-hard Ole Miss or Baltimore Ravens fans. Beyond that, I kind of thought that most people would feel like they knew me and my story, and another book coming out was just overkill.

But I wrote it anyway because I wasn't really too concerned with what critics might say. I really just wanted to talk to the kids who might be in my shoes ten years ago and the families who want to help them. If my book sold a few thousand copies and got into the hands of some troubled teens, then I would consider it a success.

I was completely unprepared for what happened next.

First I started receiving requests for interviews with some of the evening programs on the major networks. Then *USA Today* told me they wanted to run a story about the book on the first page of their Lifestyle section, the same day it was released. At first I was a little bit terrified. I'm naturally pretty shy, and the thought of getting drilled with questions for an hour in front of a camera or a microphone was the last thing I wanted to do. But I knew this was something I had to do, so I agreed.

Not only were all the reporters nice, they seemed to be honestly interested in what I had to say. Some had seen advance copies of the book and were very positive about my message. As those interviews went on, I started to think that maybe the book would get a bigger audience than I had counted on at first, but I still wasn't ready for what happened once it hit the shelves.

The first week it was out, *I Beat the Odds* hit number six on the *New York Times* bestseller list. The second week it hit number three. The publisher had arranged for me to do a few book signings around Baltimore, New York, and Memphis. When I arrived at each location, the stores were packed and the lines were literally out the door—even on a snowy February night in New York City! More than once, the store actually sold out of books, but no one got angry. People just came up to me to shake my hand, take a photo, and thank me for sharing my point of view.

I had the opportunity to meet one of the young women whose letter appears in chapter nineteen of this book. She and her adoptive family drove from a different state to come to a book signing in Maryland. We got to visit for a few minutes in private, and just getting to talk with her and her family face-to-face about our shared struggles and the hope she'd found in my story was one of the most real moments I'd ever experienced.

At another book signing, a group of students from a local charter school came by on a field trip and talked to me about how they were looking to my example as a pattern for going after their own life's goals. They did their school cheer for me in the middle of the bookstore and I couldn't stop smiling for the rest of the night.

Person after person came up to the table at every event and told me how happy they were that I had been willing to share my story in my own words. It completely blew me away.

Now, as the book is going into paperback, I am excited in a different kind of way. At first, I had really wanted to stress the fact that I didn't write this book for myself but for all the kids out there like me who need a voice. Seeing how many have already been affected by it has floored me; knowing how many more might read it now that it is in paperback is even more overwhelming. I'm starting to realize, though, that maybe writing this book helped me, too, after all. People I've known for years—former teachers, family friends, coaches—they've all told me that I've grown through this process. People tell me I sound more confident when I speak now, that I carry myself differently.

I have to admit I think they are right. I didn't notice it at first, but as time went on and the book continued to get positive reviews, I began to feel as if a weight had been lifted from my shoulders. I had looked back into my past, relived some very painful memories—and moved on. Rough times don't have any power over me anymore; I don't have to be afraid of them because I have turned them on their head—and I've shown other people how to do that, too.

In chapter twenty I wrote: "It's true that we can't help the circumstances we're born into and some of us start out in a much tougher place than other people. But just because we started there doesn't mean we have to end there." Throughout this whole experience, I have started to realize just how true that really is. Life is always about maturing and becoming a better version of yourself. Even after you've beaten the odds, there is still room to grow. I know I have, even over this past year.

Because the truth is that we are all fighting against the odds in one way or another. Whether you're an inner-city kid trying to fight your way out of poverty; a student trying to achieve despite being surrounded by a culture that glamorizes failure; a family trying to change someone's life; a teacher, coach, or mentor trying to reach out—or an adult who still carries scars from the past—we are all fighting an uphill battle. But with each step we take, we learn a little more, grow a little stronger, and gain a clearer voice. We owe it to ourselves and to the next generation to keep taking those steps.

PROLOGUE

I felt myself breaking into a sweat as I walked up to the doors of the Department of Children's Services office, and it had nothing to do with the fact that it was summertime in Memphis. I never would have dreamed a dozen years ago that I would walk willingly up to those doors. To me, they seemed to stand for everything that had gone wrong in my childhood, every bad memory, every feeling of hopelessness and loneliness and fear. And now I was headed inside.

It was a different office from the one I remembered. The big state government building downtown was the one that always stayed in my mind, and that was where I thought I was headed until the directions I'd been given had me turn into an old strip mall lined with a payday advance center, a grocery store, and a lot of potholes in the parking lot. I'd driven past this shopping center I don't know how many times in my life and had never really paid that close attention to what all was there. That afternoon in July, as I drove up for my appointment, I just circled past the stores in my car, looking for a place to turn back out onto the road because

I knew the directions had to be wrong. But then I saw the familiar DCS logo on the glass door toward the end of the mall and I knew I was in the right place.

Suddenly, I lost about three feet and two hundred pounds and became a scared little kid again.

I was a few minutes early, but I was ready for this to happen. There was no use sitting in my car to kill that time. I had come here as part of my work to write this book and I had an appointment to meet, for the first time in my adult life, the woman who spent years as the state's caseworker on my file. I needed to go in while I still had the nerve, so I parked and walked to the building, past all the other cars parked outside, past the waiting room full of plastic chairs, and up to the little reception window that looked kind of like a bulletproof barricade that you see in convenience stores in the worst parts of town.

"Hi," I said to the woman checking people in. I had to duck down so she could see my face through the glass. "My name is Michael Oher and I'm here to meet with Ms. Bobbie Spivey."

"Ooh! It's so nice to meet you!" she almost shouted. "Come on in! We've been expecting you! Ms. Spivey's office is back here."

A security guard opened the door and led me through a metal detector and back into a big room full of cubicles and offices. As I walked to the conference room where our meeting would be, a number of women crowded around—all DCS workers—and said hello or told me how much they enjoyed the movie *The Blind Side*. I shook hands and said hello, but none of the faces looked familiar.

And then, all of a sudden, I saw her. There was no mistaking who she was. I was face-to-face with the woman who had been one of the scariest people in all of my childhood.

"Hello, Michael," she smiled, giving me a hug. She barely

reached the middle of my chest as I bent down. "You look so different. You're a lot taller. And your complexion is better."

I had to laugh at that. She looked different, too. I couldn't believe that the woman I'd thought of for years as a relentless "bounty hunter," always chasing down my brothers and me and trying to take us away from our mother, was really just a tiny, pretty woman with a nice smile and a gentle voice.

We sat down at a table as we went over the rules of our meeting. Any kid who has been in the custody of the state has a right to their information once they become an adult. However, when there are siblings involved, it makes things a little more complicated because the law only allows me to get information about my own life and not about anyone else's. She explained that rules like that have to be there to protect people's privacy, so there might be some questions I would ask that she wouldn't be able to answer. I understood. I was just happy to have a chance to finally start to put together the pieces of all of the memories I hadn't let myself think about for so many years. Sean Tuohy said one time that one of my strongest gifts was my ability to forget. He was right. I had needed to forget a lot of stuff in order to not get swallowed up by the hurt and sadness. But I had finally decided that the time was right for me to start remembering.

I DIDN'T WRITE THIS BOOK JUST to revisit Michael Lewis's *The Blind Side: Evolution of a Game*, and it is not meant to be a repeat of Sean and Leigh Anne Tuohy's book *In a Heartbeat: Sharing the Power of Cheerful Giving* (which was released while I was working on this one). Lewis's book was originally aimed at football fans who were interested in some game strategy and a personal story about it; the Tuohys' book was designed to help carry on a discussion with people who had seen the movie about our lives and were inspired to find their own way to give.

My book is as different from the other two as they are different from each other, and I have a couple of goals that I'd like to accomplish with it. The first is that I want to help separate fact from fiction. After the movie came out, there were a lot of people asking me if my life was exactly how it was shown on screen. Obviously, the moviemakers have to make artistic choices to tell the story in the best way, but some of the details, like me having to learn the game of football as a teenager or me walking to the gym in November wearing cut-off shorts, just aren't true. Since so many people seem interested in these details, I hope that I can help to make a little more sense out of it all for them.

My second goal with this book, and the much more important one, is that I want to talk about—and to—the nearly 500,000 children in America whose lives have been so rough that the state has determined they're better off being cared for by someone other than their parents. The odds are stacked against those children. Less than half will ever graduate from high school. Of the ones who drop out, almost half of the boys will be imprisoned for violent crimes. Girls in foster care are six times more likely to have children before the age of twenty-one than are girls in stable families. And of those kids, more than half will end up in foster care themselves. The outlook is pretty bleak for kids like me.

I beat the odds.

Most people probably know my name from *The Blind Side*. What they probably don't know—what no one knows—is exactly what happened to me during my years in the foster care system, the years before *The Blind Side* picked up my story. The things in my life that led up to it; the way I tried to fight back; the emotions that overwhelmed me and left me confused, scared, and alone; all of the memories that no one was able to bring out of me; everything in my life that came before the happy ending— those are the things I want to discuss. All of that, and I want to provide a voice for the other half-million children in the foster care system who are silently crying out for help.

But the one thing I particularly want to stress is that I was determined to make something of myself, and that's the hope I want to offer to those children and teens, and the adults in their lives who want to help them. This book is designed to tell my story while explaining the lessons I learned along the way and looking at the mind-set I had to succeed, with or without anyone else's help.

I've read some newspaper articles recently where Leigh Anne Tuohy is quoted as saying that I would either be dead from a shooting or the bodyguard to some gang leader if I hadn't been taken in by their family. I think that had to have been a misquote because despite the sensationalist things that make for a more dramatic story, what my family knows and what I know is that I would have found my way out of the ghetto one way or another. Failure was not an option for me.

Any person who would suggest that I would have ended up facedown in a gutter somewhere is missing a huge part of the story. *The Blind Side* is about how one family helped me reach my fullest potential, but what about the people and experiences that all added up to putting me in their path? As anyone in my family will tell you, they were just part of a complicated series of events and personalities that helped me achieve success. They were a huge part of it, but it was a journey I'd started a long time before. And it's that journey I want to share in this book for other struggling kids who are fighting for their own way out.

I've tried to be as honest as I can about the things I discuss here. This book is everything I've never spoken about to *anyone* before, and a lot of things I've tried to forget. People used to say that my ability to forget was what allowed me to move on. They were right. But no kid ever truly forgets when they've experienced neglect, abuse, and heartbreak. And now, I think I can only succeed in accomplishing something meaningful and important in my life if I share those memories so that other people can learn and understand what growing up is really like for kids like me.

I have to admit that I don't remember all the details of my childhood. I have done a pretty good job of blocking them out. To finish this book, I went home to Memphis and, with the help of Don Yaeger, talked to some of the people who played a role in my childhood—foster parents, teachers, caseworkers.

To get out of that world, I did have to forget. To get to the next place in my life, I had to face what I left behind.

What started as a survival technique—my dream of getting out of the ghetto—has become a source of hope for countless children and families across America. Every week I receive boxes of letters that tell my story all over again. They come from kids in the foster system who dream of finding a family. They come from families who open their homes in the hopes of helping those kids reach their potential. They come from teachers and mentors and parents and social workers who want to make a real difference in someone's life. They come from adults who were in the foster system themselves as kids—some now have a family and a career . . . and some are now in homeless shelters or prison and wish they could start over again.

It is my goal with this book not only to tell my story in my own words, but to encourage anyone who is a part of the system or who wants to be a part of helping children out of it. Not only will the book give tips and suggestions for reaching out to kids who need help, but will also include a chapter that lists a number of local and national groups determined to provide a better chance for kids like me, who want so badly just to have a shot at a normal life.

And just what are our odds at a normal life, after a childhood shuffled between an awful family life and the foster care system? Not too great. Only about one-third of children eligible for adoption in the foster care system ever end up with parents or permanent legal guardians, and the majority of those are children under the age of eight. After that, the chances of being adopted are lower than remaining in the foster system, and continue to drop with each birthday. About 25,000 kids age out of the system each year. They turn eighteen and suddenly they are on their own, whether they have graduated high school or have a place to live or not.

Think about these statistics:

- 70 percent of kids who age out of the foster care system at eighteen say they want to attend college, but less than 10 percent get a chance to enroll, and less than 1 percent of those who enroll ever graduate.
- Within a year and a half of aging out of the system, close to half of all former foster kids are homeless.
- Children who have been taken to live in the foster system are twice as likely to suffer from post-traumatic stress disorder than are American military members returning from war zones.

I'm not just using an old expression when I say I beat the odds. What happened to me with finding a loving and supportive family was an unusual and unlikely situation. I got the chance to become something because I had a desire to break out of my neighborhood, and because there were people around me who took that dream seriously.

The ending of my story is unique, but the beginning of my story is, sadly, far too common. It is my desire to use the blessings in my life as a way of speaking up for the other children like me—for all the other Michael Ohers out there who want so badly to succeed at life but simply don't have the tools or the advocates to help them better themselves.

In many ways, this book is a guide to life, a look at how I made it to where I am today. I want to talk about the goals I had for myself that helped to break me out of the cycle of poverty, addiction, and hopelessness that had trapped my family for so long—and the people who helped me get there. I went from being a homeless child in Memphis to playing in the NFL, and that doesn't happen just by wishing for it. I want to offer advice and encouragement to both the adults who want to be part of a solution and to the kids who might pick up this book and believe there is no way out for them. Yes, the ending of my story is unique, but it doesn't have to be.

I knew when I made it to the pros that I had done the impossible. I can't say that I was never going to look back, though. That's the point of this book—to look back to all the other kids in situations like mine, where no one has any hope for them or gives them a shot to make it out of high school and into mainstream society. We don't have to end up on the streets or in prison just because the statistics say that's where we're headed.

I know there are many people out there who have the love, energy, talents, and resources to make a difference in someone else's life. It might seem intimidating at first to try to figure out how, where, and who to help. I want this book to help give some advice and direction for anyone who wants to be a part of the solution.

The numbers can seem overwhelming, and it can be hard to imagine that anything you have to offer could possibly make a difference with so many kids in the foster system and stuck in terrible neighborhoods and bad home situations. But you have to remember that every small act of love and concern makes a difference to that child.

And as I have learned, a lot of tiny gestures of kindness can add up to something great.

After *The Blind Side* came out, I had all kinds of people asking me questions about what my life had been like before I started at Briarcrest Academy. Some questions came from reporters. It didn't really bother me that I didn't have much I could share with them. But then those letters started coming in: to the Baltimore Ravens' office, to Ole Miss, to the Tuohys' house. The more I thought about the kids writing me, the more I realized that I had a responsibility to look into my past and really think about what had happened and what had helped in my life to give me hope for the future. It wasn't just time for me to be honest with myself about what I had been through; I owed it to all those other kids who looked at me and saw a role model. Kids who were in the same place I was just a few years ago were watching me not just because they liked the movie or enjoy watching sports. Sure, a lot of people write to me wanting to talk about football. But the letters that truly stood out to me were the ones from those kids whose stories I understood. They weren't writing me for an autograph. They were studying me because they wanted to learn how I had managed to make something out of my life when all of the statistics and studies you read point to kids like us having no shot.

So that was why I was sitting at a table with Ms. Spivey on a hot July afternoon, talking about stuff that happened a decade or more ago. I had decided to write a book that reached back before my happy ending to look at what happened to me and how I ended up where I did.

It was scary for me to think about opening up. I had shut down a lot of my memory for a reason. But I was also interested in being able to draw a line that would connect a lot of things I kind of recalled and to make more sense out of some of the confusion I still had about it all.

Mostly, though, I was genuinely excited about figuring out what lessons I could share about making a better life as a kid with a past like mine. I knew that I wanted this book to be more than just a story about my early life. I wanted it to be a guidebook for kids like me and the adults who want to help them.

I always felt as a kid that God had something special planned for my life. Now I know what it was. It wasn't to make me a professional athlete; it was to make me a role model for kids who, like me, are missing that person in their lives. He wanted to use me to show the world anybody can be successful, no matter who they are or what their history is. But I had to trust in that plan and be an active, real part of making it happen. I had to believe that it was possible even when it seemed it wasn't, and work for it even when it seemed pointless.

I did, and I think that's what made the difference.

CHAPTER ONE

Begging and Bumming:
Life in Hurt Village

You're not poor if you know where your next meal is coming from.

That's one of the first lessons I learned growing up. The lines were pretty clear: There were people who had food, and there were people who had to scrounge. Most of the time—way more than most of the time—I was in the second group.

I think about that now, whenever I sit down to dinner at a nice restaurant or open the refrigerator in my own home, which I always make sure is full. If I pass a homeless person on the street, I try to be pretty generous with what I drop in their cup because I know how it feels to be sitting in their spot.

It's crazy now, as I look at my career and the opportunities I have, to think about how I was living just a few years ago. I had to beg for anything I needed; now I have everything I could possibly want.

But before my happy ending, there was a very sad story.

I THINK IT IS IMPORTANT, before I talk about my life when I was little, to explain how it was when I remember it best. It's going out of order a bit, but I think it will help put everything else in context. In order to understand my life, you have to understand my world.

Like most kids, when I was younger I didn't really understand that my life was not normal. It wasn't until I had a chance to see how other people lived that I realized that the way my family lived wasn't the way everyone else lived. A child can only understand what he or she sees on a daily basis—that's what seems normal. And until I saw another way of life, the things that I was surrounded by seemed totally normal to me, so the problems with it didn't stand out in my mind.

But from the time I was almost eleven years old to the start of high school, I called Hurt Village my home. There were some foster places mixed in, but Hurt Village was always what I considered home. The name fit—Hurt Village. It seemed like everything and everyone there was hurt, broken, depressed, beaten down. And by that point, I was finally old enough to understand that it was a pretty bad place to be and a pretty bad way to live. It was all I had, but I knew I wanted something better. In some ways it looked like every other housing project in every city in America: rows and rows of identical brick buildings that were two or three stories high, busted screens and broken windows, a place empty and boarded up every few units, rusty handrails on cracked concrete steps, broken toys and broken lawn chairs in the little patches of grass outside each door. Even the air smelled greasy, dirty. It was the kind of place that depressed you instantly if you took a wrong turn and ended up driving through it. But most outsiders never drove through it because it was also the kind of place you took a U-turn in the middle of the road to get out of if you ended up there accidentally.

There were some empty lots where the kids played sports during the day and where drug deals probably went down at night, but they were my favorite places to be. Up in the front of the neighborhood was a park—not the kind with swings or a slide or anything, just four soccer goalposts that probably didn't even have nets in them most of the time we lived there. Toward the back of the neighborhood, closer to our house, was the Green Lot. There was a blacktop for basketball (where we always played by street rules, which are not as formal—or consistent—as league rules), plus a couple of open, grassy areas there; my best friend, Craig, and I laugh now about the fact that the areas probably weren't meant for kids to play in. But that didn't matter to us because in the neighborhood, we kids came up with our own set of rules for the fields: The smaller lot was the Regular Season Field and the larger one was the Play-Off Field.

We followed the NFL's schedule, so it was always exciting when we made the switch over to the big field in January. If there were older kids playing on the Play-Off Field, though, we would wait until they cleared out. A bunch of eleven- and twelve-year-olds can't really challenge seventeen- and eighteen-year-olds for playing space. A lot of times, though, we would play with the older guys—some even twenty-one or twenty-two years old. I think they enjoyed running around and knocking into people just as much as we did. We played full-tackle football, but there wasn't much blocking; everyone pretty much played receiver, running out once the ball was snapped and hoping you could catch it if the quarterback threw it your way. Each team's QB would get to the count of ten to throw the ball or run with it. Anything beyond ten Mississippis would qualify as delay-of-game. I don't remember that we ever pretended that we were one NFL team or another—we were our own team, I guess: the Hurt Villagers.

When we were still kids, a made-up team was something great to be a part of, but as we all became teenagers, something else started to appeal to a lot of boys more than football. There were gangs and everything that goes with them: gang turf, gang thugs, gang fights, gang wars. The Vice Lords and the Gangster Disciples were the two big ones I remember. If you saw big cars roll up with the leaders inside, you would scramble to get inside the house unless you wanted to risk getting caught in the crosshairs. All-out shooting matches were pretty rare, but I do clearly remember one time watching a baby get shot in the midst of an argument.

The most scared for my own physical safety that I ever was as a kid was when I was eleven years old, and the gangs had an all-out shoot-out in the middle of the neighborhood. We were just playing outside when the guys in red (the Vice Lords) started shouting at the guys in blue (the Gangster Disciples)—or maybe it was the other way around. I didn't pay attention once they stopped yelling and the bullets started flying instead. We just all ran into the nearest house, kept away from the windows, and prayed that the walls were thick enough to keep any stray shots out.

But that was my neighborhood and most of the people there didn't know any other way of life. They knew it wasn't great, but they didn't do much to change things. People who were born there usually never left except to go to another project—or to prison. Life in Memphis ghettos didn't really have its ups and downs. It was pretty much the same—all downs all the time. There would be exciting moments like shoot-outs or arrests, but as far as the big picture—the way people lived and died—that didn't change much from generation to generation. And, unfortunately, that's probably the biggest problem for anyone who wants to get out.

The history of public housing in Memphis has always been

pretty bad. At first, the developments were racially segregated by law. Because so many slums had grown up along the river during the Depression, the downtown area was getting very run-down by the end of the 1930s. The city decided to demolish a lot of those neighborhoods with plans to put real homes instead of shacks in their place. The goal was to make those houses and apartments safer and cleaner places for the poor residents of Memphis—and almost all the African Americans in Memphis were poor.

After World War II, the city put up a couple of different neighborhoods just for black people to live in. There were places like Castalia Heights, which at the time was called the "South's No. 1 Private Negro Apartment Development." It provided low-cost homes for more than four hundred families. There were also places like LeMoyne Gardens and Klondyke Arms, which were built during the 1940 and 1950s. The goal was to keep black families away from the white ones, so the poor white housing projects were completely separate. There were a lot of those, too, but at the time there were still laws that restricted where in the city black people could live. For most of the 1960s, there was a halt on all public housing, so no new projects were built then. But the population kept growing, and many discrimination laws were still in place, which meant a lot of black families literally had nowhere to go.

Racial tension was a big problem in the city, and the housing situation was a major part of it. Groups like the Black Panthers eventually got involved when other protests didn't bring about any change. They staged "live-ins" where they would occupy housing units to bring attention to the shortage of available places and the bad conditions of the existing ones.

Hurt Village started out as one of those housings projects

that was originally built for poor white people in the 1950s. But that changed as Memphis did. The unfair housing laws finally were defeated as the schools were integrated, and by the 1970s, there wasn't a white person to be seen in Hurt Village. They'd all moved out as the new laws allowed black families to move in. I guess when you're that poor, you hold on tightly to your identity because it's all you've got, so the neighborhood went from one kind of segregated to another.

Some of the other projects stayed just as they had been built. LeMoyne Gardens has always been a black neighborhood, first by law and then just because that was who continued to live there. But it changed, too. At first, it had been designed to be a place where lessons on hygiene and job skills and parenting were offered as part of a community outreach effort. But as time went by, many of the hardworking families were able to get out and buy their own homes. They were usually replaced by people who weren't as motivated to make good life choices. By the 1980s, LeMoyne had to be put under a curfew and "foot patrols" by police officers who would walk around all night because of the drug deals and high crime. It was that way in a lot of places, black neighborhoods and white ones. The people who really cared and worked for success almost all eventually left for better neighborhoods as opportunities opened up for them, and the people who replaced them in the old neighborhoods didn't have the same sense of pride or vision.

The crime problem kept growing and finally, in the late 1990s, someone decided that in order to fight the crime problem in Memphis's housing projects, they'd knock most of them down and spread the residents all over the city to new areas. The idea, I guess, was to break up the "problem people." Many condemned homes were fixed up. Others were taken down completely. By the end of 2001, more than 3,500 apartments in eleven of the biggest projects had been closed. Robert Lipscomb, the executive director of the Memphis Housing Authority, said in an interview that the goal was to "deconcentrate" the population of poor people and help move them to better neighborhoods. He explained, "I think if we eliminate some of these problem structures, we will also reduce crime."

It was a nice thought, but all it managed to do was to spread crime to new areas.

The first HOPE IV neighborhood, which is what the city called the new effort, opened where LeMoyne Gardens used to be. It got knocked down to build a mixed-income neighborhood with some middle-class homes and condos and some public housing apartments. That started a trend that you can see all over the city now. Hurt Village ended up as part of that movement. It got bulldozed not long after LeMoyne did. In fact, a lot of the places where I lived growing up have been knocked down and replaced with shiny-looking buildings and beautiful middle-class homes with shutters and big porches. But for a large chunk of my childhood, one of the ugliest and most dangerous parts of the city was where I felt the safest because it was better than the alternative. At least my family was there . . . most of the time.

My mother did her best. I have to give her that much. When she was sober, she worked hard to give us a good home and look after us. The problem was that she wasn't sober much. When she got back into her old habits, life at home kind of fell apart. We didn't always have a roof over our heads. Sometimes we'd get kicked out of one place and just wander over to another. If one of us kids had a friend who would let us stay longer than just a night or two, we'd sleep there until my mother got another place, and then we'd eventually make our way back to the new place to live with everyone else again. Once, seven of us kids lived in a car with her for about a month. We piled on top of one another to sleep, kicking and hitting one another trying to carve out a little space of our own.

We managed to stick it out, though, because we all loved one another. Neighbors used to comment on how attached the Ohers were to their family, and they were right. We truly were loyal to one another. I loved my brothers and sisters so much that I was always determined to look out for them and wanted to live as near to them as I could. I loved my mother so much that it hurt even more when she would relapse with her addiction, because I knew how much damage she was doing to herself and to our family.

Social workers would come over for visits, to evaluate how we were living, how my mother was doing, what the condition of the house was like. They would ask us questions and make notes on their clipboards. They wanted to make sure we were still going to school and not getting into trouble. We told them whatever we thought they wanted to hear because we didn't want to end up separated again. That had happened before and I think we all hated it too much to risk it again.

Besides, things could be good at home. When my mother was off drugs and working, she would remember to buy groceries, and there would be a mad scramble to grab whatever you could before anyone else got to it. If you put anything down, someone else would grab it immediately, so you learned to eat fast. It wasn't the best system, but at least we were together. Those were the good days. But they usually didn't last.

One of the first things you learn in the ghetto is to look forward to the beginning of the month, because that's when you have money. Paychecks from work come at the very end of the month and government checks come at the very start, so for the first week or two, life is good. There is no sense of saving money because when your future is that uncertain, you just live in the moment and let tomorrow deal with itself.

It was the same in my house, except that a day or two after the welfare check arrived, we knew that there was a pretty good chance that the door would be locked when we got home from school and my mother would have disappeared.

She'd often spend a couple of days gone—no note, no good-byes—but we knew why she'd left and we knew what we had to do until she got back. She was buying crack, and we had to fend for ourselves. But we never worried too much, because the beginning of the month was good for everyone, so we would bum food from other families, and maybe even bum some old clothes.

My brothers and sisters and me—there's a total of twelve of us, five boys older than me and then my younger siblings, some who were born while I was in middle and high school—learned the routine fast. We'd wander over to a friend's house at suppertime and then just stay, sleeping on the sofa or the floor until the next day. We'd go by the house to see if our mother had come back, and if she hadn't, we'd just find somewhere else to get food and crash for the night. Begging and bumming was just a way of life, whether we were living in Hurt Village or had gotten bumped to another project.

What I didn't know while I was wandering around the streets of Memphis, just north of downtown, was that I was right in the middle of one of the most important areas in black history, in Southern history, in American history. This was the area where Martin Luther King, Jr., gave a number of speeches. This was the area where he was shot and where he was taken to the hospital. This was where he had died. But if anyone had tried to tell me that as a kid, I wouldn't have cared—not because I wouldn't think it was important but because I didn't know who Martin Luther King, Jr., was.

If it didn't happen while you were living in the neighborhood, it didn't happen. History didn't matter. The rest of the world didn't matter. All that mattered was here and now, making it to the next temporary job or the next government check. Making it to the next day.

I sometimes wonder if that isn't what made me so different from the people around me. As you'll learn, my sights were set on the future from the time I was seven, and then even more as I became a teenager. Instead of getting caught up in what was right in front of me, I always seemed to have my eyes on what was ahead. Some people, if they got a little money saved up, would go and spend it on a fancy purse or flashy jewelry or brand-name clothes. No one seemed worried about saving for a rainy day or starting a college fund. It was as if the future just didn't exist for them. But it did for me. I knew that I wanted a life outside of the 'hood and I knew that the only way I could get it would be to go after it on my own.

Now, as I look back on what life in Hurt Village really was like, I realize how blessed I am to have gotten away. Sometimes people tell me that the odds of me making it out were pretty slim. They weren't slim—they were anorexic. Kids like me usually don't get to see their dreams come true. It's sad, but it's true. Happy endings just don't happen in the ghetto unless you're willing to make them yourself.

The odds are stacked against kids with rough home lives. In the inner city, fewer than half of us graduate high school. Of those who drop out, about three-fourths are chronically unemployed, and by their midthirties, 60 percent have spent time in prison. Things look just as bad for young women. Only about one-third of all teenage mothers graduate high school and 80 percent end up on welfare. Teenage pregnancies are highest in inner-city areas, but it's not just an urban problem.

In fact, anywhere you look, in any neighborhood or any school in America, there are kids who need help and hope. If you're an adult who wants to help a kid in foster care or a tough situation, the first step can be showing them that there is a different way of living from what they've always known. By helping a student focus on the future and sincerely believe that working toward their goals will pay off, you will be helping them take that first step in being something different and breaking away from the circumstances that have such a strong pull.

If you're one of those at-risk students and you want out, you have to work for it. Success isn't just handed to you; it's something you have to earn. No one can do it alone, so you have to keep an eye out for friends of good character and mentors who will give you guidance. But the way out starts with you and your determination to become something better than your circumstances. Just because your life begins in a bad place doesn't mean it has to end there.

The odds are stacked against you, but you can't let that be an excuse. You have too much promise to let the odds beat you. It can be done. I beat the odds, and so can you.

CHAPTER TWO

Life at Home

M y first memory—the furthest back I can reach to recall a time in my life—is of walking down the side of the highway with my brothers when I was about two years old. We were looking for shelter because the house was locked up again. I don't remember any details beyond that. I don't know how far we had to walk, where we ended up, or if we ever ended up finding a place to sleep that night. I just remember walking and I remember cars speeding by.

I've asked Marcus about it (he's my oldest brother and would have been about ten years old at the time), but he told me it happened pretty often that we'd get locked out, and he would load up the five of us boys and move us all somewhere safe. So really, it could have been any one of those times.

In some ways, I guess that was kind of a symbol for what most of my childhood was like: I was trying to get somewhere better than where I was, while the rest of the world rushed by not noticing me trudging along in their direction but without any real guidance.

That was how it was from as far back as I can remember: my brothers and I, fending for ourselves. Marcus was the oldest, then Andre, Deljuan, Rico, Carlos, and me. There was another baby at the time, my brother John, but my mother kept him with her wherever she went. Most of the time. But once my sister baby Denise came along, John would wander around with us, too, and my mother would carry her instead.

Being the oldest, Marcus acted in a lot of ways like both a brother and a dad to us, looking out for everyone and trying to take care of us the best he could. He did his best to make sure we all had food, brushed our teeth, showed up at school— but there's only so much a ten-year-old can do. All of us siblings loved one another a lot, but I don't think I fully realized just how much fell on Marcus's shoulders until I was much older. No matter how hard he tried, a kid can never be a replacement for a parent. Marcus didn't ever try to discipline us, but I know if he had, we never would have listened. I think we could all feel the absence of a strong male figure in our lives, even though we never talked about it. That's a hard place to be: growing up as a bunch of boys without anyone around to show you how to be a man.

I never really knew my real father, even though I met him a few times, mostly between his prison terms. My mother's brother, Gerald, had been his cellmate during one sentence, and when he was released, the man who would become my father stopped by the house to say hello to Gerald. That was how he ended up meeting my mother. They would have two children together, me and my sister Denise.

As I was growing up, he was never around. Once he gave me a few dollars when he stopped by to visit my mother, and I thought that was pretty special. He seemed tall to me then, but looking back now I realize that was just because everything seems bigger when you're a kid, since you're so much closer to the ground. In reality, he wasn't very tall at all. Physically, I seem to have taken after my mother instead of him. She is tall and pretty wide, too.

But other than a couple of short visits when I was little, that was just about all the contact I ever had with my father. None of my brothers or sisters really knew their fathers, though, so as far as I could tell I was maybe one of the luckier ones since I had at least gotten to meet mine. It may not seem like much, but it was enough to shake me up years later in high school when I learned he'd been killed. He had never been a part of my life, but he had still been something I could call my own.

I called him my father; I never called him dad. It takes more than a handful of visits and a few bucks to make a dad.

ALL TOLD, THERE ARE NINE BOYS and three girls, but we never all seemed to be in the same house at the same time. Rico, especially, I remember was almost never home. He was always out on the streets, hanging with his friends and sleeping at whatever house he ended up at that night, but almost never ours.

The girls kept to themselves. For one thing, they were a lot younger than us and my mother was usually toting one or more of them around because they were just babies when I was in elementary school. Denise, the oldest girl, is named after our mother and she is my full sister. The rest of the kids had a variety of different dads, though we all shared the same last name. It didn't matter what the father was named or what the birth certificate said because my mother decided that she wanted to go back to her family name, and from that day on, we all went by the last name Oher.

I didn't pay much attention to the fact that we were all pretty much only half-siblings, because we all looked out for one another. Once we got a little older, when we'd scrounge for food or places to sleep because my mother had left and locked us out, we would usually work in pairs or small groups. Even when we were fending for ourselves we tried to stick together.

No one in my family—not my mother or my brothers or my sisters or my grandmother—no one ever said the words "I love you." I never once remember hearing that as a child. But even though the words were never there, I could feel the bond that connected us all together, and I knew it was strong.

It wasn't that our mother didn't love us, or that she was physically abusive. It was just that sometimes she seemed to forget that she had children and that we needed her care, so she'd go off for a while and we kids would be left to take care of ourselves and one another. Since we didn't know any other way of life, we just adjusted to it the best way we could and always tried to back up one another. And we weren't the only kids in the neighborhood who lived like that. It probably shouldn't make me feel better that there were other families with the same kind of messed-up routine as ours, but back then I think it made me feel less alone and a little more normal.

My mother is from Memphis originally. I don't know much about her life, but I imagine she was like most of the people who lived around us: She was born in the ghetto, and that's where she stayed. I don't know what her schooling was like, where she went, or how many grades she completed. Those weren't the kinds of things she talked about. I do know that she was, and still is, one of the nicest ladies you would ever want to meet—when she's clean.

There would be stretches when she'd get off drugs, straighten herself out, and get a job. It was great to be home then because she would always have a smile on her face and just make you feel happy. Since she is a big lady, it's impossible to miss her in a crowd; and with her huge grin and strong hugs, she makes you proud to know her. If one of us kids brought over a friend who needed some food or a place to stay, she'd welcome them in, even though we didn't even have room for all of us, let alone for an extra body or two. But she made room. That was just how she was. She was big-hearted and loved to have her family around her.

But she seemed to love the crack pipe even more. Crack and cocaine were her drugs of choice and she never seemed to be able to get very far away from them. Every time she would pull herself together, fight back against the addiction, get a job, and try to make a nice life for us, it would only be temporary. Before long she'd be back on drugs and back to disappearing for days at a time.

To her credit, I will say that she never did drugs in front of us kids. She always made sure that she was somewhere else when she got high. She would leave to meet her friends, lock the front door, and just not come back until she felt like it. It might be hours or it might be days. It was pretty bad getting locked out of our own home, but it was probably better than seeing her and her friends all strung out.

We moved around to a number of different places when I was younger. My mother couldn't seem to hold on to any place, even in the ghetto. We lived for a while in a housing project in North Memphis called Hyde Park. Parts of it have been redone, but it was and still is one of the most dangerous parts of the city. We got shuffled around to lots of different units because my mother couldn't stay current on the rent or bills or just keep the place from getting condemned. We went without power a lot. We were homeless and living under a bridge for a couple of weeks. That was pretty awful.

When I was four or five, we lived with my grandmother Aeline, my mother's mother, but we didn't stay there long. She was the meanest and dirtiest woman you'd ever want to meet. Her house was just depressing and everything seemed to be covered with dirt or garbage. It probably wouldn't have seemed so bad if we'd at least felt like she wanted us there, but it was pretty clear that she didn't. I don't even know why she let us move in. She screamed and hollered at us all the time, yelling hateful things at my mother and at all of us kids . . . with one exception. My grandmother really loved Marcus. Maybe it was because he was the oldest and listened better—I don't know. All I remember is that she couldn't seem to stand the rest of us, but as far as Marcus was concerned, she couldn't do enough for him. The rest of us weren't jealous, though. We were actually a little relieved. If she was gushing over Marcus, she couldn't yell at us. We were all afraid of her, so the less time we had to deal with her, the better.

IT FELT LIKE EVERY TIME WE MOVED, we kids ended up at a different school. I can remember going to five different elementary schools by the time I was in second grade, and I'm probably forgetting a couple. And it seemed like no matter where we went, there were guys who could show us how to get into trouble.

Trouble was the biggest source of entertainment for the kids in my neighborhood. I think it was the favorite of some of the grown-ups, too. Almost everything we did for fun seemed to involve some kind of rule-breaking, whether it was jumping the fence of a closed court to play basketball or missing school to hang out. Of course, when I was that little I couldn't really get into a whole lot of serious trouble. But my brothers could. Rico was definitely the best at finding ways to have run-ins with the cops, but everyone seemed to have a way to find things to do that definitely were not the best decisions.

I remember being not quite seven years old and watching my older brothers Deljuan and Rico break into cars for joyrides. It never hit me at the time that what they were doing was wrong because they never stole the cars to sell them or to keep them; it was just something to do. You would steal a nice car, drive it around for a few hours for fun, and then leave it somewhere on the side of the road for the cops to find and return to the owner. They didn't see it as a crime but as a challenge. The point wasn't to actually take the car from anyone for good, but just to see if you could outsmart whoever drove it or designed the security. And, as far as I knew, it was totally normal for a kid my age to be hanging out, watching people smash windows or pop locks. My brothers and their friends let me come along on the rides sometimes, and so I thought it was totally normal to run from the cops, too. It was cool. The big kids included me, and what little kid doesn't want that?

The boys in the neighborhood weren't the only ones who didn't want to play by the rules, though. My mother was pretty good at finding trouble, too. Like I said, she couldn't seem to remember to pay our bills, so sometimes we didn't have power or water wherever we were living. She didn't always pay rent, either, so we got evicted a lot, too. But it never seemed like it was that big of a deal, and she definitely never seemed embarrassed by it. For us, it was just a way of life.

It seemed there was always a reason we had to move somewhere else, always a new school where I had to try to figure out where they were in their studies. Nothing ever seemed to change, no matter where we went. It was just a big circle for my brothers and me. All in all, it was a pretty miserable way of living, feeling like you could never really relax anywhere just knowing it was home or even just feeling safe and cared for. But at least we were miserable together.

When I was six, we ended up in a tiny duplex a little farther south in the city. From the outside, it seemed like a step up from the projects or my grandmother's dirty place. There were a couple of trees around, which made it feel nicer, and it had a little yard. It was on a pretty quiet street with only about four or five other little houses. Most important, it wasn't public housing. It wasn't in Hyde Park or any of the other projects in that area. It was a real house that we could call home in a real little neighborhood that wasn't government-run. I thought it was beautiful.

Once you got inside, though, it was pretty clear that we weren't exactly living the dream. The front door opened into a small living room where we had a bunk bed pushed against a wall. There was one little bathroom, a small kitchen, and a tiny bedroom. Nine of us were living in a house that was less than five hundred square feet.

I learned later that in most houses, people have their special places around the kitchen table, and when the family sits down to eat together, the food on your plate belongs to you; the food on somebody else's plate belongs to them. That wasn't the case with us. We didn't have a kitchen table. When my mother bought groceries, she would make normal dinners, just like any other family, but there weren't any rules on how we ate. We would all just jump on whatever food was around, and if you weren't quick enough, you lost out. The same was true with those bunk beds in the living room. They belonged to whoever happened to be the first ones to fall asleep there that night. We looked out for one another when we were out on the street, but at home it was every man for himself.

Whenever our clothes started to get dirty, one of us kids would fill up the bathtub—we never owned a washing machine that I can remember—and would scrub them by hand with a little soap before rinsing them and hanging them up to dry. You washed your own clothes and we all did our best to keep ourselves as clean as we could.

I don't remember exactly how long we lived in that house, but I remember turning seven there, so I think it was at least six months, which was a long time in one place for my family. And as nice as it seemed at first to have some open areas to play, it turned out that our neighborhood wasn't really the best place to be running around outdoors. Across the street was an empty field that was actually just a dumping ground for people who didn't want to pay for garbage removal, and then a little farther beyond that you could see a big truck farm, where all kinds of eighteen-wheelers would park to collect their loads and then drive off to wherever they were headed. The air always smelled like diesel and you could hear the high-pitched sound of the brakes squeaking whenever they pulled up or drove away. Sometime after we moved away, that truck farm was bought and cleaned up by one of Memphis's biggest businesses, Federal Express. It's now a much nicer-looking facility. It's funny to think about that now, since FedEx was one of the major financial backers of *The Blind Side* movie, and here, one of its trucking hubs is just a few hundred yards from one of the places I remember most clearly from my childhood.

It's hard to imagine that that little house could have looked any rougher than it was when we lived there, but I visited it recently while writing this book and I was shocked by how small it felt, even with the walls kicked in—because now it's just an abandoned crack house. I had to duck going through each doorway, and my head was just a few inches away from the ceiling, which is the only thing about the house that is still pretty much intact. The wall that divided our part of the duplex from the one next door is all gone and the sheetrock in each room has been smashed to pieces. All of the plumbing has been stripped out of the walls and there are empty bottles of Colt 45 thrown around the floor. The yard is full of old trash and broken glass that's been grown over by kudzu. When we lived there, my brothers and I tried to at least keep our little patch of grass clean.

But two things were still exactly how I remembered them: the back door leading out of the bedroom and the tire shop on the corner. I'll always remember them because they were major players on the day my world was turned upside down.

CHAPTER THREE

The Day They Took Me Away

n the first or second grade, kids should be bonding over Match-box cars and action figures and playing tag. That wasn't the case for me and the way I connected with my family. Because we shared that strange bond of being neglected, I think my brothers and sisters and I were especially afraid of being split up. It was like we knew—even if we didn't understand it—that the system had already failed us, and would fail us again, so we didn't want to lose the one thing we had together.

As far as we knew, the foster care people were the bad guys. We had a sense of us-versus-them, and whenever we recognized one of them coming around to our house, we would all start get-ting scared.

There was one woman who we were especially afraid of: Bob-bie Spivey. She was a no-nonsense social worker in Memphis who always seemed to be snooping around, talking to the neighbors, asking questions about our family and living situation, and trying to figure out what was going on.

There was another lady from Child Protective Services,

named Bonnie, who was in charge of checking up on my family before Bobbie took over our case. I don't remember much about Ms. Bonnie except that she was tall and would visit each week or so to see how things were at home. Before too long, though, I think she got promoted to another job, and that's when Ms. Bobbie took over—and when things started to change.

No matter where our family moved, she tracked us down. She was like a bounty hunter. Sometimes she would come to the house three times a week on what they called "homemaker visits," in order to check up on the situation in the house, to see if my mother was still clean and that there was food in the refrigerator and that we kids were going to school. On a few of her visits, it was clear that we'd been left alone for a day or two. We were terrified of those visits because we knew that sooner or later, she wasn't going to be leaving by herself.

Of course now, when I look back on it, I realize that she genuinely cared about our well-being and our safety. She didn't want us having to live in terrible conditions or missing out on an education. She had our best interests at heart and was fighting to give us a chance. But as kids, all we could see her as was the lady who was going take us away from one another. So in our minds she was just someone mean who didn't want our family to live together.

I don't know who first called the authorities about our family. It might have been a neighbor who knew we were getting left alone a lot. It might have been a friend's mom who was tired of us coming over for food or a place to sleep. It might have even been one of my mother's cousins who called. She had a couple of family members who were always worried about how we were living, though when I was a kid I just thought they were busybodies.

I wonder sometimes, though, if it actually was my mother

who had called. I wonder if she had just realized she couldn't take care of us—that we were too much for her and she felt overwhelmed and figured it would be better if we stayed with someone else, or if she just wasn't in the mood to be responsible for us anymore. I know that she loved us and wanted to keep us with her, but sometimes it seemed like she just knew that she wasn't up to the job of feeding and looking out for so many kids, so maybe she handed us off. If that's the case, it may sound like a terrible thing for a mother to do to her children, but in some ways it could also be the kindest thing. I mean, if she couldn't take care of us, at least she wanted to get us to someone who could, even if it meant we had to be apart.

We'll probably never know who first reported us; Tennessee law protects whoever makes the call to report a family. I guess that's in case it's a teacher or a neighbor, they don't have to worry that an angry family member will come after them to try to get revenge. But once a PCO (protective custody order) is issued, it doesn't matter who made the phone call. It means that there is enough documented abuse, neglect, or endangerment that the authorities have legal permission to take the children away and put them in court-ordered care. We knew Ms. Spivey had that PCO, and we knew what it meant for us, even if we didn't know who had first picked up the phone to call her.

And, honestly, it didn't matter to us at the time. Our biggest concern was making sure that we stayed together as a family. Marcus used to pull together little family meetings where he would go over the game plan for when the authorities came to take us away—because we knew it was going to happen sooner or later. Each time Ms. Spivey would make a visit, we were afraid she would be coming right back with the authorities, so Marcus had come up with a way to keep away from them and he wanted to make sure that we all knew exactly what we were supposed to do. As soon as one of us spotted the cars, our job was to yell to alert everyone else, and then to run as fast as we could in every different direction, just trying to get as far away from the house or as well hidden as possible. There was no way they could catch us if we scattered because they would not know who to go after. We'd meet up again a few hours or a few days later when the coast was clear.

He didn't want anyone to panic or be scared and forget what they were supposed to do when the time came. We knew we couldn't just pretend not to be at home. We had to do something much more drastic. We viewed our plan as a way of fighting back against the mean people who wanted to break up our family. I guess in some ways, it was the first playbook I ever learned.

In early June of 1993, getting close to the end of my first-grade year, we were all sleeping in the tiny duplex where the family was living at the time. If I remember right, all us kids were there: Marcus, Andre, Deljuan, Rico, Carlos, me, John, Denise, and Tara. My mother had left two days before and there had been no sign of her since then, and as usual, she hadn't left any food for us. She had, though, left the girls this time, even though little Denise was not quite three and baby Tara was only fourteen months old.

It was a school day, I think, but we were at home. I don't remember who first spotted the cars pull up, but there was a big window in the front room and we all peeked out to see the big car and the people in suits who stepped out onto the curb. There was no mistaking who it was. No one else in the neighborhood wore suits during the week.

Thanks to Marcus's family meetings, we all knew exactly what we were supposed to do. We ran to the back door and jumped down the steps even as they were knocking at the front door. Everyone ran a different way, hopping the fence and just getting as far from the house as they could while trying to stay out of sight. From the back door, I ran to my left toward an old body shop and tire store on the corner. It was a two-story building, and I don't know how I got up there, but I have a very clear memory of lying flat on the floor to catch my breath, and how proud I was that even though I was one of the littlest brothers, I'd remembered my job and had been fast enough to get away. And then I realized what had happened. The plan to run had been between us boys. We'd never even figured in the girls because our mother had usually taken them with her because they were so little. We had left Denise and Tara in the house.

There were a couple of windows facing our yard, so I crawled over to one to look out of it. I think there might have been some old curtains up that I kind of hid behind so that no one could see me. Sure enough, they were carrying my sisters out of the house, down the steps, and loading them into the car. They had caught John, too. All three of them were crying. They were scared and confused about what had just happened—why their big brothers were suddenly gone and who these strange people were who were taking them away from home.

All of our planning hadn't mattered. The grown-up world had won anyway. I could see Denise's face clearly in the car window as they drove off and all of the pride I'd been feeling just a few seconds before was gone. As their big brother, I was supposed to protect them and I'd failed.

AFTER THE SOCIAL WORKERS STOPPED looking for us and left, we went back to the house one at a time. It was probably a couple of days before we were all sleeping there again. It was getting into summer break, so there was even less structure to our lives now that school was out.

I don't remember when my mother finally returned, but not long after that we moved again. My memory is a little bit hazy here as to the exact timeline, but I'm pretty sure it was at this point that we lived at the Salvation Army shelter near the bus station for about a month before we moved to a little place in northeast Memphis. The shelter is closed now, but I have a very clear memory of staying there for several weeks. I think the people in the Salvation Army might have even been the ones who helped my mother find the new house and make arrangements to move us there. Whatever the case, we lived in that house for most of the time I was in second grade.

During that time, John, Denise, and Tara were put into the foster care system. Rico was put into state custody, so he was kept in a more heavily controlled environment than just a foster home. He was always the one out on the streets more than the rest of us, so if someone was going to get picked up by the cops, it would be him. But we figured that they were going to get all of us sooner or later, and we were right.

About a year after they got the little ones, the DCS people caught up with the rest of us at school. Carlos and I were at Coleman Elementary, an old brick and cement building that was two stories tall and probably felt old from the first day it was built. It was getting toward the end of the school year and everyone was excited for summer vacation to get started. One of the school secretaries came on over the loudspeaker in our classroom: "Would Michael Oher please collect his things and come to the front office?"

I was excited. The only time anyone was called to the front

office like that was when their mom had come to take them out of school for the rest of the day. That seemed like a pretty good deal to me. I was hoping that was the case, anyway—that my mother was doing well, maybe even cleaned up from drugs, and she was picking us up from school as a surprise. Deep down, though, I think I knew what was really going on. We were about to get evicted from our current house and my mother, it turned out, had checked herself into a drug treatment and rehabilitation program. She wasn't going to be home for a while, and there wasn't going to be a home to go back to anyway, since we were getting kicked out. We couldn't run and hide from the authorities forever. If they couldn't get us at the house, they'd just find us somewhere else.

Sure enough, when I got to the office, Ms. Spivey and the DCS people were waiting, and they walked Carlos and me out to the big car that was waiting for us. Grown-ups always got their way. We just had to make do with whatever decisions were made for us.

CHAPTER FOUR

Life in the System

After more than twenty-two years of working for the
department and several hundred children, Ms. Bobbie
Spivey still remembers dealing with my brothers and sisters more clearly than just about any other in her career. "Certain
families just stay with you," she told me.

The questions she was able to answer for me were definitely
proof of that statement. I was amazed by how much she remembered. But, of course, there were going to be a lot of things that
she couldn't recall, couldn't share, or simply didn't know. For that
reason, I wanted to do some research into my past. I accessed all
the court records I could about my early life and time in foster
care. Unfortunately, a lot of the records were missing—most of
them, it seems. Just in the past couple of years, a federal lawsuit forced Tennessee to clean up its Child Welfare System.
After years of bad management, disorganization, and out-of-date
policies, they were forced to pretty much completely revamp the
entire department.

A lot of new people were brought in to help straighten things out and to get them running in a better way to actually meet the needs of the kids in the state instead of just shuffling papers—and kids—around. Now, the Tennessee Department of Children's Services has some great people in charge, and I think it will make a huge difference in the kind of care the kids in the system receive. In fact, Tennessee is now one of only six states in the nation that has special accreditation for how it handles children in state custody. Back when Ms. Spivey was handling my family's case, she was also in charge of about twenty others—not twenty other kids, but twenty other families. That was the normal workload for someone in her position. Now, with the new system, a social worker usually has fewer than ten family cases to manage at once. Obviously, that is a huge improvement and makes a big difference in the amount of time and energy they can give to helping each child under their care.

But sometimes a system has to hit rock-bottom before it can be replaced with something better. Sadly, I was a part of the system right before the lawsuit brought all the problems to light, so a lot of the information and records about my life have been lost. What I have been able to find, though, has been amazing to study and jogged a lot of memories I'd thought were gone forever. I've also learned some new things I never knew before about my family and what all was really going on around me when I was too little to really understand it.

CARLOS AND I WERE TAKEN from Coleman Elementary in the afternoon and brought to the home of a woman named Velma Jones, not too far away. It was a cream-colored house with burgundy shutters and a wide front porch. It wasn't very big, but it was clearly the meeting place for the entire Jones family.

Velma, or "Twin," as everyone called both her and her sister, Thelma, was—and still is—one of the most energetic and involved ladies I know. Even though she is older now and has to use a motorized scooter to get around, she is still constantly on the go, doing some kind of community work anywhere that needs her.

Each twin had several foster kids at her home. At Velma's, besides just Carlos and me, there were four boys who I remember specifically, but I can't use their names because of privacy laws. One had bad asthma and it was always a challenge for him to keep up if we were playing outside. Twin also had a biological son about my age named Aaron, as well as a biological daughter, who was quite a bit older than us. Aside from the grown-ups, I was probably the tallest kid of the bunch already, even though a couple of them were several years older than me. In all, there were nine people—seven of whom were little boys—living in one tiny house. In that way, it kind of felt like being at home. But Twin managed to keep everything and everyone in line in a way that was definitely different from anything I'd encountered before.

We had a strict bedtime and chores to do, like washing the dishes and making sure our beds were made and our rooms were clean before we left for school. My new school was Shannon Elementary, just a few blocks away from Twin's house, so we could walk there each morning. It was a redbrick building and looked like pretty much every other school I'd ever attended, but it felt bigger because it was all on one floor. It was kept neater-looking than most of my other schools, but it had kind of a saggy look to it, almost as if it was tired from years of serving the neighborhood.

Twin was strict about making sure that we always went to school. She taught GED classes at the community center, and she was very focused on education because she saw what people had to go through as adults if they dropped out of school when they were younger.

That was tough to get used to at first—getting ready for school every morning. Carlos and I had never had anyone stay on top of us like that to make sure that we were out of bed, finished with homework, and on our way to school in time for the first bell. When we lived at home, school was much more optional and homework wasn't even a consideration.

Every day after school, we would have to catch a bus to day care, where we would stay until Twin was finished with work. That was a big challenge for me because even though I was only seven years old, I had been spending time out on the streets, fending for myself and learning how to handle myself around the older kids. It felt like an insult that I was suddenly expected to spend time in after-school day care, when I already kind of viewed myself as an adult. I think Carlos felt the same way. That arrangement continued the whole time I lived at Twin's house, and I don't think we ever really got used to it.

School and supervision after school weren't the only things she was strict about, either. Every Sunday morning, Twin loaded all of us boys up and we headed off to church. "You might be foster children, but you are God's children, too," she told us. And I guess she wanted to make sure that God had no grounds to complain that He didn't get visitation rights, because we started with the seven a.m. service, then Sunday School, and then stayed through the eleven o'clock service. It was a long morning. Sometimes, one or more of us boys was even roped into working as an usher, handing out church programs and opening doors for people as they came in.

We sang in the choir for a while, too. As part of the music program, you could learn to play the recorder or the triangle and then everyone would perform in church. We all wore robes, which was good because even then I was bigger than most of the other boys in the house and definitely all the other kids my age. The robes were very forgiving in terms of fit, so I was able to blend in with everyone else. We sang all the time with Twin, even when we weren't in church. She and Thelma were always teaching us church songs, spirituals, Gospel music. They also taught us folk songs, like "If I Had a Hammer" and music from Up with People, that super-positive group of college kids that tours all over the country.

On weekends, sometimes we would sell newspapers on corners and at stoplights on busy roads, which is a popular thing in Memphis, and other weekends we'd go camping. The Twins would load up all of their foster kids into an old trailer that was parked in Velma's backyard, and we'd drive out to somewhere just outside of Memphis and enjoy the outdoors. They had some old bikes that we took along and we'd ride those around. Those trips were a fun treat because they gave us a chance to see something other than the city. I think they were a treat for the Twins, too, because we'd always play so hard we'd completely wear ourselves out and be pretty calm for a day or two after getting back.

The rules and discipline that Twin had in her house were important for me to see because I had never lived with that kind of structure before and it definitely took some getting used to. The first few nights I lived with her were very tough because I was so mixed up about how fast my life had been turned upside down. I wasn't just in a new house and away from most of my family, but I had a whole new way of thinking to get used to, with chores and schedules and discipline and rules even about things like bedtime. I'm glad to say that she told me I never got in much trouble at her house or in school, but I didn't obey because I was happy about the way she ran her house. I followed the rules because I was afraid that if I didn't, something terrible would happen. Back in the old neighborhood, I'd seen kids get smacked around and screamed at, so even though my mother took the other extreme of no rules and no real emotional response to anything at all, I knew that physical abuse was real and it was common.

Now I understand, of course, that Twin definitely wasn't the kind of woman who would beat a child. But back then, she was a stranger to me and I sure didn't think that she loved me. After all, who could love a bunch of kids they don't even know who get dumped on their doorstep? That was what I believed at the time, anyway, and I think a lot of kids in my situation feel the same way.

IN MY CASE, I FELT LIKE EVERYONE who was involved with my care was part of a bigger plan to keep me away from my family, and that hurt. It seemed that they didn't like me—otherwise, why wouldn't they let me be with the people I loved? I felt betrayed, and I had a hard time trusting people because it seemed like all of the adults, the authority figures, just did what they thought was best without ever asking me what I wanted or what felt right for me. I saw that Twin had two biological children of her own who lived with her all the time, and I didn't understand why they got to stay with their mom while I didn't. The difference between the way she looked at them and at us foster kids was tough for me to deal with. I felt like I would always be several notches below in her mind, when all I really wanted was to have an adult love me completely.

Twin did her best to make us feel welcome in her home. She would allow my mother to come over and visit with Carlos and me whenever she felt like it. (My mother went to rehab for a while, and once she got out she moved back to the same neighborhood.) Our old house was only a few blocks away, so the first afternoon we were at Velma's I ran home to my mom, but she took me right back to Velma's house. Some of my brothers were staying in foster houses nearby, too, and we'd all meet up on Velma's driveway to play basketball or just hang out. Apparently, we weren't supposed to have any contact with family members in between our supervised visits, but Velma told me she couldn't keep my brothers away, or my mother either. And she could tell by watching us when we were all together outside that we all truly loved one another, so she didn't see the harm in it, as long as she kept an eye on everyone.

I loved our family time in Velma's yard, but the real supervised visits could be a challenge for me. Twice a month, we were allowed an official visit with our mother at the DCS office building on North Main Street. I got to know that building well. All of the foster parents of my brothers and sisters would drive us over to the building, where our mother would be waiting with snacks for us. It was like a big family reunion. We had two hours to run around and play together—and with the nine kids who were there at that point, plus a baby our mother may have had around that same time, it was a pretty noisy time.

My mother did a good job of showing up to almost every visit over the couple of years that we were in state custody. Right at the beginning there were one or two that she didn't make and never gave a reason for, but I think it was probably because she was mad at Ms. Spivey for one reason or another. When our foster families couldn't take us to the meetings, the department would arrange to pick us up. It took three or four cars to transport all of us to the building and it was really a pretty huge undertaking.

I know it caused Ms. Spivey a lot of headaches, and I think my mother knew that, too. After those first few absences, she was almost always there and did her best to make sure that we all had a great two hours together.

As much as I loved those visits, they were hard for me afterward. I would hang back and not say a whole lot as I watched everyone else laughing and running around. I preferred to just watch everyone and lock those images into my mind. In some ways, I think it was harder for me to have just a little bit of family time and then have it jerked away again. It felt like I was getting teased twice a month, being reminded of what had been taken away from me. Every night after one of the visitations, as I lay in bed back at Velma's, I would cry myself to sleep, trying to understand why we couldn't just be together like that all the time.

What I didn't know at the time was that across town, Ms. Spivey would be crying after each visit, too. When I asked her about what she thought of my family, all those years before when we were still kids, she told me that it just broke her heart to see how much we all loved one another and how obvious it was that we wanted to stay together. She said it hurt her so much to think that she couldn't get through to me, to show me that people truly cared about my best interests and wanted me to feel happy and hopeful about life. I guess she could see on my face how badly I wanted my family back together again.

In the meantime, though, the court system was making certain I would never get my wish. My grandmother was offered custody of all of us, but she said she only wanted Marcus. After about six months, though, she decided that was too much, too, and Marcus was sent to live in a group home until he "aged out" of the system. That meant he would turn eighteen, become a legal adult, and the state would no longer have to worry about him. One by one, the same decision was made about each of my older brothers. It was ruled that the goal would be for each one to age out of the system by staying put in the stable place they'd been placed by the state rather than returning home to live with our mother and the kind of life that they would have there.

Things were different for the girls, though. We learned that there was an effort to make my little sisters eligible for adoption. That meant that the courts had no hope that my mother would even get her act together long enough to make a safe home that they could be returned to, and thought that it would be best if she just gave up her parental rights for the little ones so they could have a chance to find homes with permanent families. There was another baby or two that had come along by then and been taken away by the state, and I know at least one of my little sisters was adopted by a family member on her dad's side.

With my big brothers aging out and my younger siblings possibly joining other families, I found myself right in the middle of those two groups.

The legal term that everyone kept using was that custody would be "awarded" to one person or another, but as a kid that always struck me as strange. As far as I could tell, there was no "award" involved; it felt more like a punishment than a celebration. And I was stuck wondering what was going to happen to me.

It was a strange place to be, mentally. I wished every night that things would go back to being how they used to be, with my whole family living together. But at the same time, now that I had gotten a chance to see that not everyone lived the way I had thought was normal, I knew that there was something broken about life as I had known it. Pretty soon, I got used to living with strict rules, but even quicker than that, I got used to regular meals and having a bed to sleep in. It may not have been a fancy mattress, but it was better than the floor. I started to feel pride when I would bring my finished schoolwork in to class the next day and when I started earning better grades on assignments and tests. I might never get used to having to go to day care after school, but the rest of the new things in my life were good, and I knew that I wanted a life more like this and less like the one I had known before.

But I also knew that just wanting something was never going to be enough to make it happen. I was tired of letting other people make the decisions for me. I knew what I wanted and I decided to try to get it the only way I knew how.

CHAPTER FIVE

Running Back

A nd so I became a runner. Runners are kids who leave
foster care and head anywhere else—sometimes it's back
home, sometimes it's to a friend's house, and sometimes
it's just to the streets. I just wanted to get back to my mother, to
try to pretend that the normal life I wanted so much was waiting
for me there.

Since her home wasn't far away and I was already getting
close to five feet tall with long legs, it wasn't a difficult thing to
get there. I would just take off from Velma's yard when no one
was looking and head over to my mother's place. Sometimes she
would be there and sometimes she'd be nowhere to be found.
It was never too hard to track her down, though. There are no
secrets in the projects. Everyone knows everyone else's business,
good, bad, pleasant, or ugly.

A couple of times I just sat by the front door and waited for
her to return. It was tough to know how she would react when
she found me there. At times she would grab me by the arm and
march me right back over to the house I'd just left. When that

happened, I think she must have been at a place emotionally where it was a relief to her that we were in someone else's hands. It seemed like she thought if someone else had us, then we were getting looked after, fed well, and had a roof over our heads. It was more than she could guarantee when we were with her.

But other times, she would give me a big hug and let me inside. We would stay there at her house for as long as we could. I say we, because sometimes Carlos ran with me and one of our other brothers might be there at the house, too. Most of my older brothers had been placed in group homes rather than with families, and I think that might have given them a little more freedom to come and go. Or maybe they ran, too. It didn't seem like anyone was keeping close tabs on us. Those times, when my brothers would be there, were the ones that made running worth it. Sometimes we would only get to stay a few hours, but a few times we were able to camp out at my mother's house for several days or weeks without anyone looking for us too hard.

Usually nothing much came out of me running away because the authorities always knew where I headed and could scoop me up pretty easily. But during those times when I had a long stay with my mother, a runaway report would be filed and the police would have to get involved. That happened three times while I was with Velma. The challenge was that my mother learned the rules of the system— that the authorities couldn't enter her residence without a court order or permit to do so. So whenever they came around looking for us while she was feeling like she could take care of us, we would not be allowed to answer the door. She would be the one to do all the talking and say that she had no idea where we were and that she hadn't seen us. Meanwhile, I remember peeping through the curtains to watch, and even though I thought I was being sneaky, I'm sure they could see me. But the law was on her side and my mother understood that, so she used it to her advantage.

Ms. Spivey ended up getting a guy named Eric to help her with our case. He was a short guy with curly hair; her hope was that maybe if there was a man working on our case, too, we'd respond better to him and look at him as kind of a role model. It was a great thought, but it didn't really work. It still felt to me like it was us versus them, and he was just another "them" who wanted to keep my family apart.

Eventually, though, I always got caught. Ms. Spivey was not going to give up easily. When I asked her about it recently, she laughed and told me it was always her goal to find us because she didn't want us thinking we were smarter than she was. Usually it was at school (when I would go) that the authorities would end up getting ahold of us. They would pull me out of class like they did the first time they took me away, and I would end up right back at Velma's house until the next time I ran. I think it even got to the point that they could predict my escapes. They almost always came right after one of our supervised family visits. My heart would hurt so badly after seeing us all together—one or two times my mother was even able to cook us dinner to eat together while we were there—and I couldn't stop thinking about how much I wanted a nice family life. The only thing I could do, as an eight- or nine-year-old, was to run, so it seemed to me like it was better than doing nothing.

THE UNIVERSITY OF CHICAGO PUBLISHED a study a few years ago about adolescents who run away more than once from foster homes.* According to the report the authors wrote on the study, children who run away from care more than once: "May be experiencing harm in their placements, missing family, receiving inadequate attention to their mental health needs, or lacking access to normative youth experiences such as sports."

I realize now that I was not alone in running away. The number one reason for why kids run was to get back to their biological family, even if they know that life at home was not a good situation. The study says, "Many youth equated being around a biological family with being 'normal,' and their desire for a 'real home' (which foster care was not, in their minds)." That was definitely my mind-set.

My situation was actually pretty close to what the researchers recommend to help cut down on kids leaving care on their own. I was placed with a sibling, Carlos, and I got to visit with my family regularly. But I still had that desire to run, partly because it felt like I was getting a say in my own life when I did that. That is also a common reason for why other kids leave.

I think it is important for any adult to understand that a child's reasons for wanting to get away from foster care might be a lot more complex—or a lot simpler—than they imagine. My social workers always seemed a little confused that I would want to leave a house where I had regular meals and was making good progress in school. What I couldn't make them understand was that I knew where I was living was just a temporary situation. As I said before, I didn't believe that anyone other than my family could love me and I would rather be hungry and sleeping on the

---

* Mark E. Courtney et al., "Youth Who Run Away from Out-of-Home Care." *Issue Brief*, Chapin Hall Center for Children, University of Chicago, March 2005.

floor so long as I knew that the people I was with would always be looking out for me. As much as Velma cared for me, I never could believe that she loved me.

Even though we never talked about love in my family, I felt it. Love is important in every little kid's life. The teachers at school often seemed frustrated by me, and Velma was a strict task master. Whereas at home no one got mad at me, no one cared if I struggled with reading. All my brothers cared about was that I was with them. That was all I wanted—to feel like I belonged, instead of feeling like a burden. Running wasn't a way of acting out, it was a way of coping with the way that my life had been turned inside out. The study talks about that, too, explaining that running is a coping method for a lot of kids.

What is scary, though, is realizing how many kids who are habitual runners end up in terrible situations. If they don't head home, a lot of them end up as victims of abuse or hooked on drugs. It's incredibly dangerous to set off on your own as a kid, going into the neighborhoods where a lot of runaways go.

I don't talk about my running to glamorize what I did. I was really lucky that nothing worse happened to me while I was out by myself—just about eight or nine years old—looking for my mother. It's actually pretty amazing that I ended up okay.

AFTER ABOUT TWO YEARS in Velma's care, the state finally moved us to another home. It was too bad that we had to leave her home because Velma had invested a lot of work in both Carlos and me. She had a basketball hoop back behind her house and would let us play for hours. She also took us to neighborhood games of football sometimes, and always said the two of us would be going pro someday. She fought for me in school, too. When I had a 17 percent average in school and they said I wasn't going to get moved up to the next grade because I hadn't been showing up, she worked with me and met with the teacher and principal. Within a couple of months, my average had jumped to 62 percent and I was promoted at the end of the year.

She wasn't perfect, of course, but Velma worked hard to be a good foster parent. With as much as I was running, though, I guess it was decided that I would be better off farther away from my mother's home so that I couldn't get there as easily. Carlos and I ended up getting bounced around to three or four other homes over the next year. That was when I learned firsthand that there are two very different sides to foster care.

There are people who become foster care parents because they want to make a difference in the lives of children who have been taken from bad situations. There are other people who become foster care parents because of the monthly check they get from the state. That's the part that people don't want to talk about, but, unfortunately, it's very real. There are some terrible people who slip through the cracks when the state is screening applicants to the system. Their care can be as neglectful, abusive, and dangerous as the situation the child was taken from—or even worse.

Together, Carlos and I landed in a couple of homes that were less than ideal. I don't remember a whole lot about those places, and I don't really care to. I just know that I couldn't imagine how anyone could think that how we were being treated was an improvement over what life had been like before we were taken away. One of those places even happened to be located right down the same street from the house we lived on when the girls and John got picked up by the DCS people. It was odd to be living in a strange and unhappy house within sight of a place where my family had once lived and, in my mind at least, been very happy.

After Velma's, we never stayed at one foster home longer than a few months, and with each house change, there was usually a school change as well. By that point I was always so lost about where we were in the textbook that I just stopped caring. There was no reason to try because I'd just end up somewhere else pretty soon and have to do it all over again. I guess the teachers figured that I was so far behind that it wouldn't be worth their time to try to get me caught up because I'd just be bounced out of their classroom soon enough.

I kept trying to run whenever I could and figured—I don't know what. That just by showing up at my mother's door maybe one day we would all magically be back together again? That by escaping my present situation I could somehow just erase the past? That if I ran enough times maybe one day DCS would get tired of chasing me and let me stay put?

I don't think the reason mattered so much as the fact that when I ran home, I got to be with my real family and not the one the state had assigned me. Finally, I got my wish to not have to live with foster families anymore, but I had been labeled a troubled kid and I ended up in an even worse situation.

CHAPTER SIX

Escape from St. Joseph's

've always been the quietest of my siblings, and I think that made me stand out to the social workers who were observing us. They misunderstood my shyness and the fact that I liked to observe more than participate. I've always been a person who studies things while I watch them; that's how I absorbed the rules and techniques of basketball and football—I concentrated on the games as I watched them on TV. That was how I was when I was with my family for our supervised visits, too. I guess most eight- or nine-year-old boys love to run and jump around, making as much noise as they can, but that just wasn't me.

During official, supervised visits, I tended to just watch my family talk back and forth and play together, because it felt more like being in a house. It was more like the old days, and it made me miss the times when we were all still living together.

Unfortunately, the DCS people who were supervising thought my quietness and the way I always stayed back a little bit was a sign of deeply repressed anger.

What followed was a lot of one-on-one meetings as they tried to get to the bottom of what they were afraid was pent-up rage. I didn't say much in those meetings, which seemed to only make things worse. I didn't laugh much, I didn't want to open up to them, and I didn't want to talk about my emotions. Ms. Spivey tried everything she could to get me to "give" as they call it—that is, to relate to her and let her inside my head so she could understand how I was coping with it all. For my part, I didn't understand why everyone kept pressuring me to talk. I thought it was pretty obvious what was bothering me, and I felt like they had the power to fix it but simply wouldn't.

When we talked recently, Ms. Spivey mentioned to me how her supervisor had a school photo of me from when I was at Gordon Elementary. The pictures were taken around Christmas, and I was in a red shirt, holding a wrapped Christmas box, which was a prop for the photo shoot. My smile worried them, she said, because it looked more like a smirk than a real smile. It seemed to them that I almost never had a genuine smile on my face. I don't think they realize that my real smile *is* a smirk. It always has been.

So while they were concentrating all their efforts on trying to get to the bottom of my anger, I was trying to figure out how to make it through each day without breaking down in tears. I wasn't mad, I was sad. I was a heartbroken little kid who was hurt and confused about everything that was going on around me and affected me so much but that I didn't get any say in at all. I wanted to cry all the time, but I held it in and just shook my head when they tried to talk to me. I didn't know how to tell them how much those supervised visits, when we were all together again, hurt so much afterward. I just kept thinking, "If we're good together and we love each other, why are they going to take us away again?" Each time we said good-bye, it felt like the day they'd first taken the little ones away. I felt like maybe I had somehow failed to find a way to keep everyone together.

But I was afraid if I told them all of that, they'd stop letting me go to the visits.

I know I used to get worked up sometimes, but it was more out of frustration than anger. Some expert might say that these emotions were the same, but to me they felt very different. I never wanted to lash out; I just felt a build-up of intense sadness that I didn't know how to express. I never felt like an angry kid, but I did feel upset because the situation seemed so hopeless, so I think that is what they were observing.

Whatever the case, Carlos was always good at calming me down. We shared a tight bond and I felt like he understood the confusion and sadness I was feeling. He was always a polite kid— when I talked to Velma recently, that was something she brought up: "You were both very well behaved and never got into any trouble." It was true. We really were good kids who weren't rude and didn't back-talk to adults like a lot of other kids at school. Ms. Spivey remarked on that, too. She said we were a pretty polite family, especially given the circumstances.

But the caseworkers seemed to worry that all that politeness was hiding something else within me. They thought that it was coming out in a physical way even if I wasn't putting the anger into words. I used to bump into things and pound my fists a lot, which the people at DCS felt was a sure sign of anger that I didn't know how to express. I can see how they could think that, but I don't think it was anger at all—I'm pretty sure it had to do with having man-sized hands as an eight-year-old. I had a huge body that was growing way too fast for me to figure out how to move with it. I wasn't hitting things because I was letting out rage; I was running into things because I wasn't sure yet how to handle my size. I was an elementary school kid trapped in a middle schooler's frame.

Because of their concern about my emotional situation, when I was ten I was moved to St. Joseph's Hospital on Danny Thomas Boulevard, near the famous St. Jude's Children's Hospital. At the time, I thought I was just being kept in a ward for kids who didn't have anywhere else to go. It wasn't until much later that I realized I had been placed there to be observed and treated for anger issues.

It's funny, now that I know better what all is there in Memphis, to realize how close we were to St. Jude's, one of the best places in the country for sick children to receive top-notch care. But our hospital was just the opposite; at least on our floor, it was filled with kids who no one seemed to care about at all. I also learned later that St. Joseph's was the hospital where Martin Luther King, Jr., was declared dead after he was shot. But I didn't know that at the time, and I don't think it would have mattered anyway. I wasn't impressed with historical stuff; I just wanted out.

The adolescent unit felt like an institution, with nurses and quiet voices and fluorescent lighting. At the ends of the hallways were keypads that required passwords and card scans. It just felt very impersonal and a little dehumanizing. At least in foster care I was living in a house. There, it felt like I was getting locked up in prison and no one would tell me what my crime was. The whole atmosphere made me even unhappier and very uncomfortable. I wanted to be home—even if that was just an old car or a tiny room. I wanted to see my mother again, even if she was going to go off on her own. I kept hoping that if my brothers were allowed home, maybe she would be happy enough to stop doing drugs.

It's interesting now to learn that I was sent to St. Joseph's for emotional monitoring because one of the things that bothered me most at the time was that I thought that no one realized I had any legitimate feelings about the situation. It felt like they thought I was just angry, or else a robot who didn't care about what happened to me. But I knew I had very serious and strong feelings: I wanted a normal life like I saw on TV. I wanted my family together in a steady place where we wouldn't have to wander around to bum a sandwich or a place to sleep at night. I had started to see that there was another way to live, and I wanted to bring that way of living to my own family.

While I had hated foster care, I also knew, even then, that it was doing something good for me. There were rules that kept me off the streets. There were regular checkups to make sure I was going to school. Despite my sadness, I had started to see what was missing from my life.

I stayed at St. Joseph's for about two weeks and adjusted to the new routine. We weren't in school; instead, we would have to talk about our feelings with adults (who I realize now probably were psychiatrists and counselors). Then when we weren't in those evaluations, we could watch television.

A funny side note from my stay there: I think that's where I got my love for movies. I am a huge fan of films, and I think it first started when I got to choose whatever videos I wanted to watch from St. Joseph's collection. I'd never had videos before, and definitely not dozens of them to choose from to watch on my own. It might not sound like much, but it is actually empowering to get to make your own decision about what movie to watch, and for a kid who felt like all decision making had been taken away, that was a big deal. I slept in a little hospital room, with my own TV with a VCR on the bottom. It felt so grown-up, so exciting to return to my own room with a video I'd picked out from the movie shelf.

As much as I loved the access to movies, though, I found myself getting bored and a little irritated with life there. I didn't understand why I was there, why I had to have endless discussions about how I was feeling and do the silly little exercises I had to do. The plan, I found out later, was to keep me for a full month and then make recommendations for my future care based on what they learned from observing me. However, I decided that two weeks was long enough. I was tired of the inaction. I wanted something to happen, to feel like some kind of progress was happening in my life.

So I started studying my surroundings again, the way I like to do, and I noticed that all of the adults seemed to be coming and going from the double doors at each end of the hallway. One afternoon, while no one was watching, I wandered down there and studied the door. Even though there were those computerized locks on the doors, it seemed to me they weren't quite shutting right. So I folded up a sheet of paper and worked it past the heavy bolt—and the door opened right up! I looked around, and no one else seemed to have noticed anything; there were no alarms going off or people running to see where the security breach had happened. Breathing heavily, I made myself walk slowly and calmly back to my room so I could come up with a plan.

I knew if I ran off then, they'd miss me within just an hour or two, since we were getting ready for dinner and then bedtime, when they did room check. Instead, I figured I would wait until the morning and slip out then. Not only would I be able to make my way home in daylight, which would be a lot easier, but I also figured that they wouldn't notice as quickly that I was missing. If I wasn't in my room, whoever was looking for me would assume I was off talking to a counselor or taking another test.

So that night I remember very clearly taking that little folded

piece of paper, kissing it good night, and putting it under my pil-
low before falling asleep with a huge grin on my face.

The next morning, I crept past the nurses' station, ducking
down so they wouldn't notice me passing by, and tried my lucky
paper again. Sure enough, as soon as I slid it past the blot the
door popped open and I slipped out the door, into the stairwell,
and then headed for the first exit I could find. I was free, and I
was heading home.

AS FAR AS I WAS CONCERNED, I was done with the DCS. As much
as I knew the meals and the structure were good, overall the
experience was bad. I was almost eleven years old and every bit
as unhappy and unsettled as I had been when they first collected
me almost three years before. I made up my mind that I was
finished with them and their "fixes" for my life. If anything was
going to get better, it was going to be up to me to make it happen.

As an adult, I now understand more about what was going on
within the system at that time, and how broken it really was. The
caseworkers were really overloaded, there was almost no account-
ability, and there were a lot of out-of-date rules kept in place by
out-of-touch people that benefited no one—especially not the kids
whose lives were being steered by them. Not to mention that there
was a terrible breakdown in record-keeping, which is clear from
the fact that almost all my files have just disappeared. All of Tennessee was in bad shape, but Shelby County, where Memphis is
located, seems to have been the worst place by far.

I don't want to sound as if I am ripping on everyone who was
involved with my custody. Obviously there were a lot of people
who genuinely cared and wanted to make a difference. The problem is that there always seem to be more children who need help

than people who are able and willing to help them. Even with the huge improvements that Tennessee's Department of Children's Services has put into place by totally rebuilding itself, life in the slums hasn't improved much. Just the fact that a state has to have a department dedicated to the welfare of its children—the fact that something like that has to exist at all—means that the problems are still there and kids are still suffering in foster care, even good foster care. That's the worst part of it to me. As long as the cycle of poverty continues, there are always going to be kids who think there is no way out and just get trapped in their parents' way of thinking and living.

Parents who have spent time in foster care have almost twice as high a rate of having their own children taken away and placed in foster care, or see their children become homeless, than parents who didn't spend time in the system. The sad truth is that even though children are being removed from bad situations, they are sometimes placed into situations that aren't much better. Or, if they are fostered with a loving and supportive family, their stay often isn't long enough to make a lasting impression that will help them learn how to make better choices with their own futures.

What happens is that the kids learn to imitate the behavior they see as normal, and as a result, they end up making the same mistakes their parents did. You would think that someone who was abused as a child would know how much it hurts and do everything they could to not do that to someone else. But instead, when they get angry as an adult they react the only way that they know how, in the way that has become natural to them. With neglect, sexual abuse, substance abuse, gang membership, with all of the ugly things that exist in the world, kids tend to go back to what they know. It's certainly not something unique to the projects, of course, but it sure is common there. That's why I ran away from St. Joseph's, just like I'd run away from Velma's—I wanted to get back to what was familiar, what I knew.

For the kids who are assigned to caring, helpful families for longer than just a few months, their lives can be completely turned around. They get a chance to see what responsible adults look like. They understand what it is like to live with rules and discipline. They learn that there is a different way of living from what gets you trapped in the ghetto. They find out that you can trust and love people who are trying to help you become whatever you want to be. It can be a long road to break down the walls of distrust, anger, or sadness that a lot of children have put up as a survival mechanism, the only way they know to protect themselves from the hurt. Loving homes that offer support and encouragement are so important because they can help reprogram what the child views as normal and okay.

Unfortunately, not everyone gets placed in that kind of home.

Just because I was able to understand some things better, though, doesn't mean I was able to make the best choices. I still don't know how my mother could treat her kids the way my siblings and I were treated. I still don't know how she could think that living with the drugs and neglect and filthiness and irresponsibility was okay. I still don't know how she thought that if she kept living like that, things would get better. I heard a quote one time from S. Truett Cathy, the man who founded Chick-fil-A. He said: "It's better to build boys than mend men." I thought that was a good statement and very true. Helping kids see a better way of thinking and living when they are young is so much easier than trying to re-teach them a whole new way of life when they are adults and end up making the same mistakes their parents made.

But it's not up to us kids to fix the world's problems. There are a huge number of kids in America who feel helpless and need stable homes right now. You can take action by choosing to help just one child. The ripple effect of that action can end up touching many lives and even generations.

CHAPTER SEVEN

"Home" Again

After all of my attempts to run and hide, when I was either brought back by my mother or the authorities, I finally got my wish to stay at home. After my escape from St. Joseph's, I was finally released from the system back into my mother's care.

Well, technically, I wasn't really released to her so much as no one came after me again to haul me away after I left the hospital. I don't know what changed my mother's status so that I was allowed to stay with her at that point, but they eventually decided it was okay and left us alone for a while. I just know that the goal of foster care is to return children to their birth families whenever possible, so that might have been what made them decide we were okay.

Judging from the last document I know of before I ended up back at home, though—a ruling filed in July of 1996—the Juvenile Court of Memphis and Shelby County had something very different in mind for Carlos and me. In that document, it says that they wanted to change my status to "permanent" in the foster care system. It seems that Carlos was targeted to just age out of it. He was almost thirteen at the time, and I guess whoever makes the decisions thought that nothing was going to improve with my mother in the next five years and that Carlos would be better off turning eighteen and then getting released without ever returning home.

I don't remember if we knew anything about the court's decisions for us at that time or not. Even if someone had sat us down and tried to explain it all to us, I think it would have gone right over our heads. When you're a kid, it seems like forever to think even six months down the road. Five years would be impossible. As far as we could tell, the longer we stayed in the foster system, the longer we were being kept away from the rest of our brothers and sisters, and we just wanted our family back.

So when I got home and no one came after me for a couple of days, I figured they might finally have decided to leave us alone— and I guess I was right. Since we weren't in any immediate physical danger, maybe the authorities just decided that it was worth another shot for us to try to live at home again. Or maybe they were tired of chasing me and figured that if I wanted to be at home so badly, they might as well let me. I didn't look like too much of a kid anymore, either. By then I was coming in around five feet seven, which is pretty crazy when you're barely eleven years old.

For all the great dreams I'd had about what it would be like when I finally got home, though, I was pretty disappointed. I'd always imagined that things would be just like they were before we got split up, with all of us kids together again, plus the new ones that seemed to just keep coming. But a lot had changed during those few years. Marcus was an adult now. Andre and Deljuan were about to be. Rico was still in the system, and John,

Denise, and Tara were living with other families. So for now, home meant my mother, me, and a new baby or two. As their situations changed, my older brothers drifted in and out, but I was facing the hard realization that things would never be the same—that we'd never all live together again.

My grandmother had moved up to Minnesota. I have no idea if I have any family up there or if there was a specific reason why she chose that particular state. But as far as I was concerned, the farther she was from us, the better. I didn't want the DCS getting any kind of ideas about moving us back in with her. She died just a year or two after I returned home for good.

I had changed, too. I had started to put the pieces together of what was required to get a life and a job outside of the ghetto someday. As much as I had hated being in state custody, I did have someone getting me up each morning and making me go to school. It's amazing what regular attendance can do for you. Even if I had pretty much given up on trying to learn much, as I was changing schools so often, I still began to understand better what responsibility was all about and why it was important to show up where you are expected each day.

There was one big change that I was especially excited about, though. When I was close to turning eleven, we moved from Hyde Park to a house in Hurt Village that had three bedrooms, and as far as I could tell, it was a mansion. We had never lived in a place that big, and even if the every-man-for-himself rules still applied at dinnertime or in terms of grabbing a place on a mattress, I thought we were living large.

That year was actually a good one. I was back home with my mother, which I had wanted so badly, and I was put in Ms. Verlene Logan's fourth-grade class at Gordon Elementary. I had missed so much school at that point, and even at eleven years old

I was much bigger than the other kids, but she never made me feel as if there was anything negative about that.

She had taught for many years and was wonderful at it. She made all of us feel special in her class and she went above and beyond in caring for her students. She could always make the rough, rowdy kids calm down with a few gentle words. She always told us that we were all intelligent and could accomplish great things in life if we didn't give up and take the easy road. She tried hard to let every student know he or she was important to her and seemed especially proud of me when I made the honor roll. I found out later that if there was ever a child who didn't have clothes or shoes that fit, Ms. Logan would quietly go out and buy them what they needed.

But I didn't know that then. I just knew that she was the teacher who was determined to make all of us in that inner-city school believe in ourselves. "Can't never could and ain't never would" she used to remind us, in order to help us believe in our abilities and the importance of working hard. She used to encourage me to keep up with sports because whenever we would play T-ball or kickball at recess, I used to tag everyone out—including her. "One day, you'll make big money because you are too fast!" she used to say, laughing, whenever I'd chase her down at first base. I loved that she saw value in my athletic talent instead of acting like it wasn't an important skill.

In fact, I saw her just recently at an annual charity event in Batesville, Mississippi. A friend of hers knew that I would be there and gave Ms. Logan a call. She came, but I don't think she thought I'd have any clue who she was. The second I saw her, though, I shouted, "Ms. Logan!" and gave her a huge hug. It was such a wonderful surprise. I reminded her that she and I shared the same birthday, and she thought it was so funny that I would remember something like that after all these years. But I don't think it was crazy at all. Each one of us has memories of a favorite teacher or coach from when we were little, and even if we didn't know how to tell them at the time how much their encouragement meant to us, we carry that memory in our hearts. I had carried that memory of Ms. Logan with me for years because she made me believe that I had a talent worth developing and the ability to see it through.

But the good times didn't last, and even the thrill of the new house wore off, too, when it was clear that nothing had really changed except our address. My mother disappeared a few times; we ended up moving again, too, staying one place for a little bit before getting kicked out of it for one reason or another. Pretty soon I was back to camping on people's floors or sofas, or even sleeping in doorways and under bridges when the front door was locked. Memphis winters usually aren't too bad, but the summers are brutal.

My mother fell back into the same routine of getting clean and then relapsing, and the same routine of neighborhood trouble started up again, too. There was a grocery store right next to Hurt Village called Chisholm Trail Grocery. It was a pretty big store where everyone did their shopping—and stealing.

I should take a second here to apologize to the owners of the store, which is out of business now, and probably because of all of the stuff I shoplifted from them. It started out as just a dumb thrill. All the neighborhood kids stole candy there, and I did, too. Not to be making excuses for what we did, but I don't think that it actually occurred to us that it was bad. After all, most of our parents weren't very active in teaching us right from wrong. And it seemed like more of a game than anything else. If you made it out of the store with your candy, you won. If you got caught, you lost. I lost four times.

But as I started getting a little older and the growth spurts started, stealing from Chisholm Trail Grocery wasn't a game anymore. It was actually a matter of survival for me. My mother didn't keep food in the house and what I was able to bum from people in the neighborhood wasn't nearly enough to fill me up. I needed food—real food that could keep up with my body. So I moved from stealing candy to stealing meals. I'd smuggle out pork chops, steak, whatever I thought I could get back home to cook without getting caught. I always tried to steal meat if I could because that was something we definitely didn't get at home.

Most of the time, though, I got food through the same old routine of begging and bumming. I'd hang out with a friend and just wait for their mom to offer me something to eat. There were certain moms who I could always count on to feed me. We all kind of knew the deal: There were the nice moms who you knew couldn't stand to see a kid not eat; there were moms who would give you something only if you asked; and there were the moms who clearly didn't want you around at all. All the kids in the neighborhood knew who was who. When she was off drugs, my mother was one of the nice ones who the other kids knew would give them something if they came by our house. Everyone loved her when she was clean because she was just such a loving woman. But as soon as she went back on drugs, it was a different story.

Things get a little fuzzy for me for a while as far as trying to remember exactly when and why we moved to certain places. I remember that this was when we ended up staying in a shelter for a few months while my mother tried to straighten herself out yet again. Then for a while we were in a housing project called Alabama Plaza, which was a bunch of old brick apartment buildings and a couple of townhouses that were all kind of smashed together. There, the main activity was to sit outside in lawn chairs and just wait for something to happen. Whether it was a fight or an arrest or a car chase, something was always going down, and you wanted to have a front-row seat for whatever it might be.

After it became clear that I couldn't bum or steal enough food to stay full, I decided to try selling newspapers again, like I had done when I was living with Velma. She used to take the kids in her care down to get bundles of papers on weekends and then have us stand on street corners selling them in order to make a little money. I had been a pretty good little salesman working for her, so I decided to give it another try. Each Sunday morning, I'd go down to the *Commercial Appeal* and get a couple bundles of newspapers, then sell them roadside at various intersections. Typically, I could make about seventy to eighty dollars, but on a good day I could pull in even more. That was enough to buy dinner for a week and sometimes even new clothes if I'd managed to outgrow what I had.

I loved the feeling of being able to do something for myself. Every week I was out with my newspapers and just about every week I sold them all. Then I could face the rest of the week knowing that I wouldn't be hungry. It became my Sunday morning routine to get up early and be out on the corner around six o'clock. Eventually, I even got promoted to one of the best corners in the area because the newspaper knew they could trust me to show up and work hard. Other people would get bored and wander away before they had finished selling their stack, but I was determined to stick it out. I made a game out of it, telling myself that if I left before the last paper was sold, I'd lose.

One day, when I was fourteen, a scary-looking neighborhood guy came up to me and said, "I know you know what this is." He was right. I did. I could see that he had a gun in his pocket—it was a mugging.

"Where's the money?" he asked. He was acting totally normal so that the cars passing by had no clue what was going on. It just looked like a man talking to a kid on a corner, but he definitely meant business.

"It's in my coat over there," I told him. It had been a warm morning and I'd taken my coat off as I walked up and down the street. I figured if I could get just a few steps ahead of him, I could take off running, but he must have known what I was thinking.

"If you run away, I'll blow your back out." The way he said it, I could tell he meant it. So I walked over to my coat slowly and pulled out the money. I was just finishing up, so I had a lot— there was about a hundred dollars in my coat because it was such a nice day and a lot of people were out. I carefully took it out and handed it over to him. He took the money and ran away.

I was pretty depressed, but at least I knew I had about twenty or thirty dollars in my jeans pocket, and he'd been too dumb to ask if I had anything else. It was going to be a hungry week.

THE DCS EVENTUALLY FIGURED OUT where I was (or maybe just finally noticed that I was no longer in their custody) and they started up with their visits again, though this time they didn't try to take me away because my mother didn't give them a chance to. From my running away adventures in foster care, she had learned the rules of the system and ramped up her refusal to let the caseworkers in the house. The caseworkers obviously knew exactly where I was, which was right on the other side of the door, or maybe just hiding in the bedroom; but the law said they couldn't come in without a court order, and so long as they showed up empty-handed, my mother made sure they left empty-handed, too.

Eventually, even those visits died down. I'm not sure what prompted the authorities to lay off, but I think it might have been some kind of arrangement to keep me in school. I have to say that it worked out pretty well, because eventually I ended up having one very good year academically.

In seventh grade, I was placed in the Ida B. Wells School. It was specifically designed for kids who were behind their grade level due to bad situations at home. I really thrived there that year. The teachers took a different kind of interest in the students' achievement and I felt like I was being stretched academically for the first time in my life. The school itself was located in the basement of Manassas High School, the local high school. We had our own sports teams, and we played against some of the Manassas squads. Even though it was a separate school from Manassas, it was in the neighborhood with the kids who lived all around me. So I was uprooted again, but our program didn't stick out as different.

That year at Ida B. Wells was one that opened my eyes to the fact that school could be a place for real learning to happen if you were taught by committed, caring people. Watching the teachers and knowing that some of them had come out of situations not unlike mine made me see the reality of making something out of your life. I discovered that's really what it comes down to: You've got to want to be something. The problem was that it seemed like there was no one else around me who wanted to be something. There was no one else who I went home to at night who was working hard with dreams of a regular job and the responsibilities of a nice, middle-class life.

After that year of school with good teachers and role models,

I was desperate for someone who could mentor me outside of school and teach me how to convert that dream into action, but I couldn't seem to find anyone. I didn't have a person who could sit down and talk me through things like planning for the future and making choices that would benefit me in the long term. So I just started to rely on my own common sense and my own ideas of what I wanted for my life. I would stop and ask myself: Is this a smart decision? What are the consequences of hanging out with these guys? What kind of trouble could I get into if I did this or went there? Do I want the thrill as much as I want to get out of this neighborhood someday?

But following through on those smart choice wasn't always easy. When I hit the eighth grade, I started as a regular student at Manassas High School. That's where I was playing. I say "playing" because that's really all I was worried about with school. I would show up for school just enough to stay eligible for sports (I was on the varsity football team as an eighth-grader, since I was about five feet eleven by then and as big as the seniors), but otherwise I would just hang out during the day with my brothers and their friends.

Looking back on it, I realize what a bad decision that was at the time, but it was just so much easier. While there were some great teachers in the Memphis city schools, after Ida B. Wells, I just didn't have any of them. Mine pretty much didn't care if I was there or not. They just kept passing me so that they didn't have to deal with me anymore, or answer questions as to why I was failing—and it wasn't just me. That was true for so many kids. We would just be held in the classroom for the period and the teacher would go over the material, but nobody (including the teacher) seemed to care if it stuck or not. No one checked for homework or book reports or even gave many tests. When no one around you, at school or at home, seems to think learning is important, it's pretty hard to think that it is important yourself—especially when you're a teenager.

But there was one period a day that I never, ever missed: lunch. At any inner-city school, you'll almost always see that the lunchroom is packed even if there aren't that many kids showing up for class. Since we were all on the free lunch plan, we knew that we would always get a hot meal in the cafeteria, so even on the days when we just stayed out on the streets, we were always in school at lunchtime.

Once the school day ended, I would head out to the baseball fields. That was the other thing I never missed: baseball practice. If I had skipped school that day, I still made sure I got to the locker room in time to head out to the field. I was the pitcher for the Manassas Tigers, and thankfully I wasn't quite so tall yet that finding a blue and gold jersey was impossible.

I know I'm not built like your typical baseball player, but I was pretty good as a pitcher. I mean, I could throw a football almost seventy yards—pack that same power into just about twenty yards and that's some heat behind a baseball!

The bigger and stronger I got, the more I started thinking about what I would do when I was grown up. I could look around me and see that there didn't seem to be any other kind of an escape. The teenage girls I knew were all starting to have babies, the teenage boys were becoming part of the gang scene, selling drugs, or both. It was as if everyone around me had given up on ever leaving the ghetto.

But I knew I was different because I had a secret—something I'd not told anyone. I'd figured out how I was going to leave the ghetto years back in 1993, when I was still in second grade.

CHAPTER EIGHT

MJ and Me

M artin Luther King, Jr., had a dream, and so does every kid in foster care. Our dreams might not be as big as his were, but they are just as important. Having some kind of a goal is absolutely essential for kids trapped in poverty and bad family situations, because if we can't hope that things might be better someday, then we basically lose a reason to live. It's a lot easier to fall down, or to stay where you are, than it is to fight gravity by trying to pull yourself up.

Having a dream can be the first and most important step in making it out of the system. It's got to be something more specific than just, "I want a lot of money" or "I want to be famous." You've got to know not just what you want, but why you want it. A goal of being rich isn't enough to make you put in the work day after day; you have to know why you want money—to buy a house, to take care of your family, to be able to always put food on the table, to make sure your spouse and kids aren't stuck in the projects— whatever it is that is your dream beyond just the surface of what sounds like an easy life.

You also have to have a sense of what you are naturally good at. For example, if you have trouble with numbers, you should work on that, but you probably shouldn't look for a career as an accountant. If you are a terrible singer, that probably isn't the best road to go down. If you're very shy in front of people, you probably should look for a different career from being an actor, even if you like movies. But maybe you're good in science class and like studying it—then becoming a science teacher might be just the right job for you. If you always get good grades on writing homework in school, then maybe you should make your dream to be an author or a journalist.

Of course it's great to dream about doing all kinds of different things, even if no one else thinks you can. I don't mean to say you shouldn't dream big, but if you are fighting against odds that say you're going to fail, you should make sure you know what your talents are, what makes you stand out, so that you can work on developing those things that make you different; because just by recognizing what it is that you're already pretty good at can give you a head start on working to make your dream something real.

For me, that dream came to me when I was seven years old.

THE TIMING COULDN'T HAVE BEEN BETTER. Right around the same time that the social workers came for us and took the littlest kids away, I saw something on TV that would change my life. It would give me something to hold on to over the next few years as I bounced around to different foster care homes and hospitals. It would give me something to keep in front of me after I returned home to live with my mother and the old patterns and bad habits came into play again. It would change the way I thought about everything else I was facing, because it gave me a goal to work toward when I started feeling hopeless that my life would never get me anywhere away from the 'hood. I watched the NBA finals between the Chicago Bulls and the Phoenix Suns and I knew—I knew—that sports were going to be my way out.

Even at seven years old, I was a big kid. I was taller and broader than the other kids in my class. I was bigger than most of my foster brothers, even though I was usually the youngest. I was almost as tall as some of my brothers who were four or five years older than me. But I wasn't an obese kid. I was carrying a little extra weight, but I was athletic and fast on my feet with my reflexes—and I was tough. I'm sure having five big brothers had something to do with my toughness. If you wanted to play with the older kids, you had to keep up and you couldn't be a crier. I had never played any organized sports, but people always seemed to think I should, so I realized pretty early on that I had a unique combination of build and talents.

I remember watching the NBA playoffs at my cousin's house. There were a bunch of us there—most of my brothers, some cousins—everyone was just packed around the TV as the Bulls tore through the Hawks, the Cavaliers, and the Knicks before making it to the finals against the Suns. I didn't know where any of those cities were: Atlanta, Cleveland, New York, Phoenix. I didn't even know where Chicago was, even though I was cheering for them like they were my hometown team. All I knew was that Michael Jordan was the most incredible athlete I had seen in my life, and the way he played ball just blew my mind.

It was late spring, which meant it was already hot in Memphis. I don't know if the air-conditioning was broken or if it was just because there were so many people in such a small room watching the game, but I felt like I was sweating as much as if I'd been out there playing with the Bulls, a feeling that probably helped to make my new dream seem that much more real to me.

The series against Phoenix had been crazy. Chicago was looking to win its third championship in a row—something that hadn't happened since the Celtics were on their streak in the 1960s—but Phoenix kept fighting back. In the first five games, Chicago scored 100 points or more, and in Game Three, Phoenix ended up winning after taking the game into triple overtime, with a final score of 129 to 121. It was nonstop action on the court and probably the most exciting thing I'd ever watched. The Bulls won the first two games, lost the third, won the fourth, and lost the fifth. I was completely hooked by how intense it was to watch these two unbelievable teams fight it out.

Then in Game Six, all of the drama came to a head. Chicago was determined not to let the series go to Game Seven, and they were leading by 11 points in the second quarter, 10 in the third, and 8 going into the fourth; but Phoenix turned up the heat and pulled ahead 98 to 94. In the last minute of the game, Michael Jordan got the rebound, drove it down the court, and scored to make it 96 to 98. There were 38.1 seconds left on the clock. Dan Majerle missed the shot for the Suns and the Bulls got the ball back at 14.1 seconds. In the best show of teamwork I had ever witnessed to this day, Jordan passed to Scottie Pippen, who passed to Horace Grant, who shot it over to John Paxson, who had hung back in the three-point zone. It was a perfect shot—nothing but net—and the buzzer sounded. The Bulls had just won the championship for the third year in a row, Michael Jordan was named the series MVP for the third time in a row, and I was now hooked on sports.

For the next few days, and then the next few weeks, I kept replaying those games (especially the final one) over and over in my head. There was Jordan, scoring at least 40 points in four consecutive games—even scoring 55 points in Game Four—and averaging 41 points per game for the series. It was unreal. No one seemed to be talking about anything else except what an amazing player Jordan was. It seemed like he was starring in every commercial and was on every piece of sports gear out there. Even in my neighborhood, where no one seemed to have money for good food or to pay bills, any kind of fancy brand-name stuff with his name or his face or that famous silhouette of him jumping was something you just had to have. His name was money.

The message was pretty clear to me: MJ was never going to go hungry. If sports could make you so famous that you could always pay rent, then that was what I was going to do. After all, I didn't see many people in my neighborhood headed to regular jobs each morning, so athletics was kind of the first real career I recognized that interested me.

Of course, it turned out that every other little boy around me seemed to have the same dream—they were all going to be either professional athletes or rappers. Some wanted to be both. Rap was a popular option because rap stars were all over TV with the fancy cars and pretty girls. There seemed to be a lot of stories about kids from the projects making it big in the rap world and shaking things up with the establishment, but I knew that wasn't really my personality. Sports was the road for me.

When I first came up with that idea, to become the next Michael Jordan, I just figured it would be something that would happen to me when I grew up. But as I got older—especially as I hit my teenage years—I started to see a difference between myself and the other kids who had my same dream. There were the kids who *wanted* to become something, and there were the kids who were *working* to become something. The ones who wanted it ended up getting involved in drugs and gangs—the easy way to some quick cash and the most common route to take. The kids who were working toward it were the ones who were

showing up to school, trying to be responsible, and studying players instead of just watching sports. It was a much smaller group.

Even though it wasn't the easier way, I decided that I wanted
to be one of the kids who was actually working toward the goal,
prepping myself for the kind of life I wanted. For me, it wasn't
about the money or the flashy lifestyle or the power. If I had
wanted that, I could have easily joined the Vice Lords or Gangster Disciples, and with my size, I probably would have climbed
up the ranks as a bodyguard and started bringing in the money
quickly. But it was a whole different way of living that I was after,
so I chose to take the other route.

I took that personality quirk I've always had of being an observer,
and I focused it on sports. I didn't just watch games to enjoy them;
I paid attention to the way the athletes moved and what the different plays were. I really *studied* the way the game was played and
the players themselves. I learned everything I could about how they
got to the pros, and by the time I was in eighth grade, I knew that I
would have to go to college if I ever wanted a shot at playing basketball or football. But by the time I got to the ninth grade, I knew that
college was not going to be an option for me.

That was when I decided to learn about junior colleges, where a
lot of these players went before going to a big-name school. If I could
figure out how to make that happen, maybe I would have a chance.
First, though, I had to figure out how to get through high school.

Yeah, it's true that I slacked off sometimes, going to school
just for the free lunch and sports practice. It is tough to show up
every day with your homework done when the kids around you
don't do it and encourage you to just hang out with them. It's
also tough to do what you're supposed to do when you feel like
no grown-ups—not even most of the teachers—even care if you
do it or not. In the end, I realized any success I might have would

come down to two things: 1) finding good people to surround myself with; and 2) taking responsibility for myself.

Not long after I moved back home after foster care, I met a kid in my neighborhood who was just a year younger than me and who felt all the same things I did about getting out of Hurt Village. That kid was Craig Vail.

Craig's dad had moved away from his family not long before my family moved into the neighborhood, but I think it helped that he'd had a male role model for at least the first ten years of his life. Craig was the middle child of five living with his mother (plus two more half-sisters), so we were similar in that we weren't old enough to be counted with the big kids but we weren't so young that we were still the family babies, either. We were both kind of quiet, and I think that's why we first started hanging out; but as we got older, I could see that there was a reason Craig and I stuck together, and it was because we needed each other. Craig didn't think the drug dealers or gang members were cool. He didn't drink or swear or do any of the stuff that was just normal for everyone else around us. He wanted to have a steady job to support a nice family when he grew up, so he was determined to do whatever it took to make that happen.

That was exactly the kind of friend I needed—someone who didn't laugh at me when I said I was going to have a different kind of life. Being with Craig reminded me that I wasn't wasting my time by studying sports, practicing my game, and trying to figure out what it would take to get me to junior college. He wasn't into sports as seriously as I was, but he was definitely focused on making a good future and responsible life for himself. I needed that kind of solid friendship to help keep me in line and my mind in the right place as I steered through the challenges of middle school and becoming a teenager in the ghetto.

But even before meeting Craig, I was determined to make sports my "thing." Somehow I knew sports would give me discipline and help me grow my talent so that I could use it as a tool for a career. I was actually the only one of my brothers who was really into playing sports. I don't mean I was the only one who liked to play—in the neighborhood, everyone plays basketball. But I was the only one who was involved with sports teams at school. It just seemed like a good way to work on my life skills, and I think I kind of knew, in the back of my head, that it would help keep me out of trouble, too. My older brothers each had their own talent. Some were good at singing, or at video games we played at other people's houses. Marcus was artistic and was great at drawing. Carlos was athletic but never got excited about playing for school teams the way I did. Athletics just became the area where I stood out—and it wasn't just because of my size.

A couple of my brothers are tall, too: Andrew is six feet six and Deljuan was six feet seven. My sister Denise is pretty tall, too. Just like my mother, she's about five feet ten, so I am grateful to our mother for passing that height on to us. But while my size may not have made me stand out in my family so much, it definitely did with my friends. Craig used to tease me about fitting in with the men of the neighborhood when we'd play football on those empty lots. But I wasn't just a huge guy—I was also very fast and coordinated. The teams I joined in junior high and high school helped me develop these abilities.

I made plenty of poor choices when it came to school. I missed far too many days and relied on my teachers and coaches not noticing or caring. What I was really doing was putting my eligibility at risk, which would have upended my dreams. But fortunately, I ended up making more good choices than bad choices.

CHAPTER NINE

Big Tony and Steve

As I hit my teenage years, I totally threw myself into sports. I was pitching for the baseball team at school and playing pick-up ball. In Hurt Village, the Greet Lot was where everyone got together to shoot hoops. I played there and at Morris Park, near where my mother had moved us as I was starting high school. There were a lot of talented players, plenty of guys who could have played college hoops, but they had no one who took an interest in them by getting them to buckle down and go to school or to learn to play with discipline.

Whatever sport I was playing at the time would be my favorite—if it was football season, then that was what I liked; if it was baseball season, then that was my number one. Unfortunately, I didn't have a chance to play on any serious teams. The middle school teams weren't much of anything, so I also played for a local church team. But things really took off for me when Big Tony Henderson showed up at my door one day.

I'd been playing ball in one of the local parks when some kids in the neighborhood talked to their coach, Big Tony, about me. There was a tall guy named Zack who played for Tony. He was older than me, but everyone thought he was my big brother because he and I were built so much alike. Some of the other kids on the team told Tony that I might be good to have playing with them as well.

Tony didn't know who my mother was, so he made some calls and a friend of his, Earl, said he'd take Tony over to our house. So one evening, Tony and Earl showed up at our door and talked to my mother about letting me play on the AAU (Amateur Athletic Union) basketball league Tony had going in Hurt Village. As it turned out, Tony had known my uncle Gerald, who they all called "Hawkeye," after a character on the old TV show *M*A*S*H*. (No one seems to remember why they called him that; they just did.)

Since everyone had told Tony that my size and speed were unusual for a kid my age, he was determined to get me as part of his team, and my mother agreed. So starting in eighth grade, I began playing basketball with the Hurt Village team, which was for middle-school-age boys, roughly fourteen and under, and took on other neighborhood teams around the city.

Tony moved me around to every position, but I preferred to play a bit out of the fray where I could just shoot baskets without having to be in the mix of players so much. I was good at hitting the basket from a distance. Refs loved to call fouls on me—every time I would get a rebound or even get close to another player while trying to guard them, it seemed that the whistle would blow. When you're as big as I was and you're playing in a league full of normal-size eleven- and twelve-year-olds, it's almost impossible not to foul. This was a challenge I would have to deal with all the way up to varsity basketball in high school.

Tony understood what it was like to be a big kid. He'd never actually played basketball himself—he'd boxed when he was younger—but he was a pretty big guy (hence the name). I think he understood some of the challenges of trying to move a huge body effectively in a game where I was literally double the size of everyone else.

Our team did very well, winning a number of tournaments in both my eighth- and ninth-grade years. We traveled all over the city, playing other teams and nearly always beating them. I loved playing in AAU. I felt with each practice like I wasn't just enjoying the game but that I was doing something that was going to make me better and help set me up for the career I wanted.

I am pretty laid-back about most things, but when it comes to something I feel is a responsibility, I get very worked up about it. If practice was at 5:00 p.m., I showed up at the gym at 4:30 p.m. I don't think I ever missed a practice or was even late. I might have been willing to slack off on some things, but sports was my future and I was fanatical about my practice and discipline.

Tony had pulled some strings to get me transferred from Manassas to Westwood High School, which was where his son Steve was going. Steve was a year younger than me, but it was a seventh- to twelfth-grade school, so we were together. Westwood technically wasn't in my district or in theirs, but an uncle let Tony use his mailing address so that Steve could go there to take advantage of the better sports programs, and Tony let me use that as my address, too. I was so happy when Tony managed to get me into Westwood for my freshman year of high school that I started going much more regularly.

I loved Coach Johnson, who was my football coach my freshman year. He made us lift weights, ran us, and focused on conditioning and training. I loved all of it, even though summer practices were especially awful. But I knew what I was good at and I knew what I had to do to get better. Coach Johnson pushed us in order to make us understand the importance of discipline. He also helped us to take pride in ourselves and our team.

Basketball was a challenge, too, because I was surrounded by a lot of kids who had been playing organized ball since they were six or seven years old. I didn't have anywhere near as much experience, but it gave me something to work on. My goal was to be as disciplined as those other kids so that no one watching us all play would be able to tell who'd been playing in a league since they were very young and who hadn't. It took a little while to get used to playing organized ball instead of just street rules, but I eventually learned.

But other than sports, I really didn't have anything in my life that I was happy about.

Life at home was still challenging. My mother sometimes would fall back into her old habits of doing drugs and leaving us alone. At that point, it was just two new little brothers and me who were still at home with her. Carlos was there for a little while, but he was nearly eighteen and moved out on his own.

My mother would come to school to pick me up a lot of afternoons, which was nice. She also came to almost all of my home games for football and basketball, and would sometimes bring some of my brothers, too. But whenever the school called her to talk about my grades, my mother was nowhere to be found. It was as if she only wanted to be involved with the easy parts or fun parts of my life.

When I talk with people now who knew my family back then, I've had people say to me: "You know, it wasn't like she was getting high and leaving you all alone every single weekend. She'd be clean for months at a time before slipping up." I understand what they're saying—that is, not to let the bad times at home crowd out the good times. But how many times is it okay for a mother to smoke crack and lock her kids out of the house for days at a time? I would think that one time was one time too many.

As a kid, I knew it wasn't a good way to be living, but I didn't have the perspective on the situation that I do now. Now, I wonder why people try to defend that kind of behavior. I love my mother with all my heart, and I always will. But that does not mean that I can just look past her actions and say it was all okay because it only happened every couple of months instead of every week.

I don't want anyone to think I am talking in a disrespectful way about my mother. It's important to honor our parents—that's even in the Bible—but honoring them and approving of their lifestyle are totally different things. I will always love and honor my mother, but that doesn't mean that I can just shrug off her addictions and pretend that they didn't hurt me or my brothers and sisters. In some ways, I feel she robbed us kids of the chance of future success, as her actions told us that selfish, indulgent, irresponsible behavior was okay.

That is probably the reason why I liked Steve's company so much; I just enjoyed being around him and his family. I liked that he worked hard, applied himself in school, didn't cut class, got good grades—all of that. I admired it because I'd never seen anyone else my own age who was disciplined like that. And other than my good friend Craig, I didn't have any other friends who were so determined to keep out of trouble.

I also liked that Steve had a father in his life. There were so few men in my neighborhood who stuck around and stayed with their families, I didn't even know what I was missing until I saw what it was like to have a male authority figure in the house. Ms. Spivey had tried to bring a male authority figure in a few years earlier with Eric, but since he was part of DCS, I couldn't see him as anything but one of "them"—the people who wanted to split up the family. But seeing a man come home every day and interact with his own family was a different story. That was when I knew I wanted that—needed that—in my own life.

Maybe it sounds strange to have had mentors who were kids, but I admired the dedication and character of Steve and Craig and I know that having them around helped keep me out of some of the more serious trouble I could have found.

One great example was when I wanted to go to the same summer basketball camp as Steve. There are all kinds of clinics all over the city for hoops skills, and the one that Steve was going to was for eighth grade and under, so I was too old for it. But I knew that when I stuck with Steve, things were good. So Tony made a phone call to someone he knew working the camp and they let me in.

It was really a good thing they did because the week I was attending that clinic, the group of neighborhood guys I some- times hung out with got caught for stealing a Cadillac from an old couple near the hospital, and they had several thousand dol- lars of stolen cash in the car, too. When the police were question- ing them, someone said that I had been with them. But when the cops did a little digging, they found out that I'd been at the bas- ketball camp and couldn't have been involved in the theft. I'd like to think I wouldn't have taken part anyway, but it was valuable to have people who could confirm that I had been running drills in the gym when the car was stolen.

But it wasn't just my company that I had to watch. My atti- tude needed some work, too. At one camp the next summer, right before my tenth-grade year, I got so fed up with the refs blowing the whistle on me when I was sure I hadn't fouled anyone that

I finally snapped and started cursing up a storm, then I stormed out of the gym and started walking home. Unfortunately, the camp was about eight or nine miles from where I was living, but I didn't care. I was so steamed that I'd rather walk that far than spend any more time with those refs and coaches.

It was toward the end of the day and Big Tony had driven over to pick up Steve and me, but when he heard what happened, he got back in his car and drove down the route he figured I'd take to get home. Sure enough, he found me trudging down the sidewalk, still mad and still fed up with the world. "Get in the car, Mike," he ordered as he pulled over. "We have to talk."

The rest of the drive, he told me how I needed to get control over my language and my emotions if I was going to succeed in school and life. He told me that there would always be refs who would call fouls on me just because of my size, but I had to deal with that and just be a better player so that it would be harder for them to do that.

The more I thought about Tony's lecture, the more I realized he was right. It occurred to me that I'd been reacting the way I had always seen people react—explosive, angry, obscene. But I had to learn how to do better if I wanted to *be* better. I had tried hard to make smart decisions on my own, but I needed reminders to keep me on track. I started looking around me and I realized that every time I had a bad attitude or lost my temper, I was just living up—or down—to the level of expectation that people had for me.

When you're a poor kid from the inner city, most people already have their minds made up about who you are and what you can or can't do. Every time you slip up, lash out, slack off, or sulk, you're just playing into their hands by acting like the stereotype they've already decided you are. Too many people have already labeled you as a "bad kid" in their minds, and if you curse or pout or act up, you're just letting them think that's all there is to you—that you're just one-dimensional, that what they see on the surface is all there is to see.

Other coaches used to say to Big Tony, "Why do you even bother with that kid? He's just a waste of your time." Some even said things right to my face like, "You'll never amount to anything. Stop kidding yourself." I'm sure Ms. Spivey heard things like that more than once, too, from people who were too fed up to see past the challenges to the potential I had.

I was lucky to have Tony at that time in my life, and it probably helped that he was from my neighborhood. I think that helped me stay open to listening to him. It was a big struggle for me to learn how to trust, and as I've gotten older and read more about it, that seems to be a pretty common problem for kids from challenging backgrounds. In my case, it seemed like just about everyone in my life who was supposed to take care of me had failed me. My birth parents failed me; some of my foster families failed me; the broken system at Child Protective Services had failed me; the judges who kept sending me back to bad situations failed me. Because of that, it was tough to think anyone could have good motives. I mean, just look at how my brothers and I saw Ms. Spivey. We thought she was a horrible woman who was trying to break up our family. We didn't realize that she was trying to get us into more stable, safer homes than what we had. It was a big deal to find someone I felt I could really trust.

From talking with other kids who grew up in neighborhoods like mine, I have found out that very often, even the coaches can't be trusted. A lot of times there are guys who coach inner-city teams just because they want to "discover" the next big pro athlete who will be their meal ticket in a few years. They aren't coaching the kid because they care about him but because they want to be able to hang around when he gets rich and famous; they call him up or come by his house for money. The kid gets used for his talent, and there is an expected "payback" for the coach. It's disgusting and pathetic, but it happens all the time.

Tony seemed to be concerned with helping me develop as a player as well as looking out for my well-being. I needed that kind of support, and I was very grateful for it. He tried to help me adjust my attitude and start thinking differently so that I would be ready for whatever opportunities high school varsity sports might bring my way.

This is a school photo from around the third grade. This is the first picture I know of from my life.

This is a school photo of me from about a year later. Leigh Anne got this photo and the one before it from a foster family I had lived with. They were both damaged, but she had them restored as a surprise for me.

This photo is from the fourth grade, the year I was in Ms. Logan's class. It's the same photo that one of our social workers had hanging in her office.

We had some family portraits taken when I was in high school. Sean and Leigh Anne also wanted some individual shots of each of us kids.

After church on Sunday, we would sometimes go out for lunch. This is a picture Leigh Anne took of me, S.J., and Collins one week at the country club.

Here I am, my junior year of high school, shooting a free throw at a basketball game.

Also taken my junior year, this is an action shot of me throwing the discus at the Tennessee State track and field meet.

My senior prom date, Alliesha Easley, played women's basketball at Briarcrest and graduated from Ole Miss.

There I am, hamming it up in my senior yearbook photo. See? My normal smile really is a smirk.

After a football game my junior year, I posed for this photo with some of my teammates. Notice the scoreboard behind us. That was a big win!

This is one of my favorite pictures. It shows my family at Collins's and my high school graduation.

On Bid Day at Ole Miss, I went to see Collins get her bid for Kappa Delta. Miss Sue, who was also a KD at Ole Miss, smiles with us.

Also from my graduation ceremony, this is Principal Steve Simpson and me.

I love this family picture at Vaught-Hemingway Stadium, the Ole Miss football coliseum. Collins and I are both freshmen in college.

Meet the Rebels Day takes place in Oxford every August before the season starts. Collins was there as an Ole Miss cheerleader, and I was obviously there as a football player. We are both sophomores.

A lot of my Ole Miss teammates would get together at my family's house in Oxford to eat after home games. Notice Miss Sue sitting proudly in the middle of all of us who she tutored at the university.

This is a shot of me in action on the field for Ole Miss.

This is me during NFL Draft Week standing on top of Radio City Music Hall in New York City.

Here are me, Collins, and S.J. in our family's 2008 Christmas card. The Rebels were Cotton Bowl bound!

Sean and Leigh Anne put on a little signing day party for me at Briarcrest when I announced my decision to go to Ole Miss.

After an All American awards ceremony at Harvard my senior year, we went over to the ESPN studios for a visit. I think I look pretty good behind that desk!

When my name was called on Draft Day, I couldn't imagine that life could get any better—especially since I was surrounded by some of the people who meant the most in the world to me: (from left to right) Jimmy Sexton, Collins, Craig Vail, me, Sean (in the back), Leigh Anne, S.J., and Miss Sue.

CHAPTER TEN

The Road to Briarcrest

reat opportunities might occasionally fall in someone's lap, but I believe you are much more likely to find one when you go out and chase the opportunity down. That's exactly what I did as I prepared for my sophomore year of high school. It seemed like there was a great opportunity for me to get a better education and to have access to better sports programs, and I was determined to jump on it.

I'd already stopped pretending that a normal life for me at home was possible. I had a place to sleep at my mother's house, but it was just a mattress on the floor. My mother was doing a pretty good job of staying clean at that point, but she wasn't especially interested in me or what I was up to and pretty much just left me alone entirely. I just knew I didn't want the kind of life she had. I wanted something better, even if I didn't know what it was or how to get it. I loved her and my brothers so much, but home felt like a hole I was stuck in and couldn't climb out of. I didn't want to stay trapped.

So instead of staying with my mother, most of the time

I was moving from house to house, sleeping with whoever would let me stay and eating whatever food they'd let me have. I finally settled on staying with Big Tony's family because they were the best example of what I wanted my own family life to be like.

Steve was one of those kids who was working, instead of just wishing, his way out of the projects—good grades, good athlete, no trouble. That's one reason why I liked staying at their house. The other reason was that they lived in a neighborhood outside of the projects. Just the fact that they were a family that had made it out—and stayed out—was a big deal to me. My mother moved us to places that weren't public housing several times, but we always eventually ended up back in the 'hood, like it was some big magnet that kept pulling us back, no matter how far away we got from it. But Tony's family was an example to me that the ghetto doesn't have to have an iron grip on a family. They weren't rich by any means, but that wasn't the point. Tony escaped the mind-set that affected many people around us. He was self-sufficient and knew he didn't have to stay in the projects just because he was born there.

Big Tony was a good coach and Steve had become a good friend of mine. I knew that if I stayed close to them, I'd have a better chance of making something out of myself than if I stuck with the thugs who seemed to be everywhere in my own neighborhood. So I started staying over at their house whenever I could. I just went home with Tony one day after practice and I ended up staying for a couple days. Pretty soon, I just stayed there all the time. Steve didn't seem to mind, although I think he was a little surprised at first that his dad let me stay over on a weeknight, but it soon just became a normal thing for us. They put some sheets on the sofa and that became my bed. I'd usually remember to take them off each morning so people could use the sofa during the day, and then I'd just spread them out again at night. Tony's family opened up their home to me, and even though it was only a temporary solution, what came out of it changed my life forever.

BIG TONY AND HIS MOTHER, Miss Betty, had kept after Steve and his brother, Tristan, so Steve's academic record was solid and his grades were good. Before she died, Miss Betty asked Big Tony to be sure to get his boys a Christian education. Tony wanted to make good on that promise, so he started looking around to see what Christian schools Steve might be able to attend for high school. Steve was a grade behind me, but I was determined to go wherever he went. If he was leaving Westwood, then I wanted to leave, too. The Henderson family seemed to understand the importance of going after opportunities, and I wanted to be a part of that.

The summer before my sophomore year, Big Tony got serious about finding a private school. One day in July, he loaded us up into his old Ford Taurus and we drove across town to the University of Memphis High School. I had never seen a school that looked as neat and clean as that campus. I couldn't believe that any school could look that nice. If I had known better, I probably would have felt out of place walking around in my basketball shorts and T-shirt.

Tony, it turned out, didn't call ahead for an appointment. He just rolled up to the school and walked confidently into the front office with Steve's records under one arm and mine—or what he could get of them—under the other. Steve and I waited in the hallway while he talked with someone inside. I don't remember how long we were waiting before Tony came back out and said we'd have to try somewhere else.

A day or two later we drove over to Christian Brothers High School, a huge campus off a very busy road near Baptist Hospital. It was the same routine: Tony just walked in unannounced, completely confident, and Steve and I waited for him to make his pitch to the administrators. Christian Brothers had one of the best football stadiums I had ever seen, and the school itself felt huge and clean and new. But the same thing happened: Tony came out of the office after a while and said we'd have to try somewhere else.

The next day we were off to Evangelical Christian School, which was out in Cordova, east of Memphis. For as big a city as it is, you can get just about anywhere in Memphis in roughly thirty minutes, and it's pretty much impossible to tell where Memphis ends and Cordova begins. But that drive felt like the longest one that we took. I had no idea where we were headed as we drove down some roads that looked like they were taking us out into the middle of the country. Finally, when we arrived at ECS, I relaxed a little bit because it seemed a bit smaller than the other two schools we'd visited, and it had a nice campus with some woods around it. At the time, it was also one of the powerhouses of private high school football for the state of Tennessee. But once again, after Tony left the front office, he said we'd have to find another place.

It turned out that what he was hearing over and over again was that Steve's grades looked promising, but mine were just too low and my records too incomplete for me to be considered. And since Steve and I were determined to be at the same school, it meant we had to keep looking.

My school records were a mess. I can't even remember how

many different schools I attended. I often changed schools when my mom moved, and I went to different schools when I was in the foster care system. Sometimes I'd just be in a class for a few weeks and then it would be off to another house and another school. My mother had never made me do homework or helped me read a book. My mother had never made me get up and go on the mornings I was feeling lazy. No one had ever bothered to take the time to find out what I did and didn't know. I did just enough work to let them know I was still alive and they passed me along because I was a good athlete, and especially in high school, they wanted to keep me eligible to play.

Finally, after a long, hot week of driving all over Memphis to visit different schools, we arrived at Briarcrest. It was a long drive out to the campus—it felt almost as long as to ECS. And when we reached it, my jaw nearly hit the floor of the car. I had never seen anything at all like that school. It was actually still under construction at the time—classes wouldn't start there until the next school year—but the administration offices had already moved over from the old campus, so that was where we headed.

Everything about it, from the buildings to the stadium, was cleaner and newer than any school I'd ever seen. I don't think I realized there was such a thing as a nicely paved parking lot without potholes and huge cracks running every direction with weeds popping through. Tony seemed excited about Briarcrest, because he'd just found out that a basketball coach he respected a lot had recently been hired there and he hoped that Steve would have a chance to play for him.

While Tony went into the office to make his pitch, Steve and I stood out in the sparklingly clean hallway. We didn't say much, we just sort of looked around at the beautiful new building, afraid to touch anything, and then looked back at each other every now and then and shook our heads, as if we were both thinking, "Who in the world has this much money?"

Tony's meeting took a little longer than it had at the other schools, so it seemed like that might be good news. But as the three of us walked back to his old Taurus, he told us that the answer from Briarcrest was pretty much the same as everywhere else: that Steve seemed like he could succeed there, but my grades were too much of a problem to let me in. What was different, though, was that Briarcrest offered us a possible solution.

There is an alternative school in Memphis called Gateway Academy, which is run by a local church and offers programs for kids in trouble or struggling badly in school to get their grades up. The Briarcrest administrators agreed that if I went there for a year and showed real improvement, it might be possible for me to start at Briarcrest the following year. It was a good enough deal for all of us. Steve could go to the new private school and I would get my grades up through the alternative school and be on track to join him at Briarcrest after a year.

That fall, we started a new routine: Tony drove Steve out to school in the mornings and I worked in Tony's body shop and studied with the Gateway materials during the day. Once a week on Wednesdays, I would go over to the Gateway campus for one-on-one instruction and to take tests on the material I was supposed to have studied on my own the week before. Their curriculum was set up this way to help students adjust to the discipline of regular school. The only problem was that I'd never even learned how to study, so I found myself looking at the books and trying to make sense of them, but feeling totally lost.

Steve was also having to work hard to stay on pace with his classes. He has always been a really smart guy, especially in math, but the level of academic instruction at Briarcrest was so much higher than at the city schools we'd both been attending that he needed a little extra help to keep his grades high. So his cousin, who was a schoolteacher in Memphis, came and tutored us in the evenings until Steve got used to the faster pace and tougher subjects and until I got my grades high enough to be considered at Briarcrest. It didn't take Steve long to get the hang of things, but I just wasn't making any progress.

I watched jealously as Steve was making friends and getting ready for basketball season. I wanted so badly to be a part of that, but no matter how much I tried to learn the Gateway materials, the more lost I got. I was overwhelmed because everyone just assumed that I'd had at least some kind of normal schooling up to that point, so they jumped right into the material and expected that I would be able to catch up quickly. I've always liked numbers, so the math courses weren't as big of a challenge as the other subjects. But the worst subject of all for me was Spanish. That was where I really had no idea what I was supposed to be learning. I'd never learned the different parts of speech in English, or how to identify different tenses or verb conjugation—or what those things even meant. And all of a sudden, I was trying to learn how to do it in another language. It was impossible. Overwhelming. Hopeless.

It was probably the most frustrating situation I had ever found myself in. I knew that this was likely going to be my one chance for a real education. What was even more important to me, though, was that Briarcrest was going to be a chance to play sports in a setting that would not only get me good coaching but also open up doors for other opportunities, like getting into a junior college. As tempting as it was to go back to my old school in my old neighborhood and just hang out, I also knew that if I did go back I would never leave. I knew I would never make it out of that part of the city and that way of living. But how does a sophomore in high school learn everything he is supposed to learn with no formal instruction—especially if he's never been taught any of the basic techniques for how to succeed?

But it was also clear to everyone that I was trying, that I was getting up every morning and working with Tony (who was also teaching me how to drive). I was also trying to apply myself to Gateway lessons for the weekly test. I hated it, but I kept at it.

You don't go through that if you're stupid and you don't work that hard if you're just a lump. I think the people around me could tell that I was driven by something and they decided that I must have wanted that education badly enough to do everything I could to try to get it, even if it looked hopeless.

Several months into the school year, after watching me fight my way through the workbooks and tests with Gateway, Tony called Briarcrest and asked them to reconsider admitting me right away. Not all of the teachers and administrators were enthusiastic about it, but they finally looked at the effort I was making and the rut I was stuck in, and they agreed on the condition that I get extra study-skills help and that I not play any sports until my grades improved. The school has a program called ESS (Educational Support System), which is for students like me with a weak foundation in academic skills. ESS was a good resource for me while I also learned things like note-taking, study skills, and time management.

And so about halfway through the school year, I suddenly found myself standing in a crowded hallway at Briarcrest, head and shoulders above all the other students who were filing past me in the hallway. All I could wonder, though, as I looked around, was if *I* was the one in over my head.

CHAPTER ELEVEN

High School

My first day at Briarcrest was overwhelming. It was already almost halfway through the school year, so there wasn't anyone else with the first-day-of-school nerves that I had.

It wouldn't be until the next year that the high school would move over to the huge new campus I'd seen when Tony took Steve and me there over the summer. As I looked around, I couldn't believe that the "old" campus was so clean and well-maintained. Everyone apologized for how crowded it was because all the grades were using the same building until the high school's big move coming up that summer. But compared to the schools I'd attended all my life, it was amazing.

Memphis has some beautiful public schools. East High School looks like some kind of a palace. It's really incredible. That wasn't the kind of city school I'd known, though. Almost all of mine were nearly identical, big, tired-looking brick buildings with tall windows that opened in five or six horizontal panels all the way down, a sure sign they'd been built before air-conditioning was standard. A teacher could tilt the panels open to catch a breeze when the classroom got too hot, which was anytime from April on. The windows only let in a dirty brown light. Whether they looked so cloudy because they were old or just needed to be washed, I don't know. I just remember that no matter which school I was in, the whole building—the classrooms and hallways and offices—all seemed to have that same kind of dull, hazy light from all of those old windows.

Looking around the hallways at Briarcrest, I noticed that everyone seemed happy. The students were happy, the teachers were happy, the administrators were happy. People seemed like they were glad to be there, and that they were glad you were there, too. It might sound nice, but it actually felt a little weird.

I am a creature of habit. I like things to be set a certain way, and I like to stick to that routine. I don't like a lot of adventure or change or to do anything that goes against the grain. I'm naturally kind of shy, at least at first, and even after I get to know someone I'm still usually pretty quiet. Especially when I'm in a new situation, I like to hang back and evaluate everything, to see how people connect with one another and react, just to get a feel for the flow of things. I would have liked to just blend in the first couple weeks at Briarcrest so I could watch and learn about how to fit in there. But from the time the teachers introduced me to the class to the time the bell rang, I stuck out. I was a giant black kid surrounded by a bunch of shiny pink kids. Not standing out was *not* an option for me.

There were a couple of other black students at the school, and they pretty much all played sports, so Steve had gotten to know some of them. Not all of them were rich, either. That helped me to feel as if I wasn't a hundred percent out of place, but the school was definitely almost all white and definitely a whole lot better off money-wise than my family. The schools of my experience had always been pretty much all minority students, and the percentage receiving free or reduced-price lunches was about the same.

Briarcrest opened in 1973, and since the Memphis schools were still struggling with integration at that time, I think it probably was established at least partly as a place for wealthy white families to send their kids. Since then, though, they'd done a great job of getting more diverse and enrolling kids of all different colors. Steve had told me that everyone was very friendly and didn't seem to have an issue with his skin color, so that made me feel a little more comfortable as I tried to figure out how I was ever going to fit in.

I soon found out that as much as I tried to blend in (pointless as it was), people were actually really nice to me. I don't think the other kids knew what to make of me at first, but soon I think they saw that I was a pretty gentle guy who was scared to death, and they started waving to me in the mornings as we walked in, or saying hi to me in class. I still didn't say much at all, but I at least knew some names and could smile back.

The dress code at Briarcrest was pretty relaxed then: Shirts had to be tucked in, pants had to belted, and boys had to be clean-shaven. It's probably good that there was no uniform because I seriously doubt there would have been anything that would have fit me; I was well over six feet tall by then, and almost three hundred pounds. Every Wednesday was a dress-up day because of chapel. The girls had to wear dresses or nice pants and the boys had to be in shirts and ties. Thankfully, Tony let me borrow some of his church clothes because I definitely didn't have any that would work.

Chapel was about forty-five minutes or an hour long, and

would start after second period. Everyone in school met together in the big auditorium and we basically had a church service with singing and a lesson and then some announcements. It was a little weird for me at first because I'd never gone to church regularly except when I lived with Velma. When I was living at home we would go every now and then, but then it was usually to ask for food or money afterward. It was nice to see so many people come together for no other reason than to worship, and I was a part of it. The service style was very different from what I had known going to church with Velma, which was a little looser and had some different music, but I enjoyed it once I got used to it. It was a nice way to pause for a little bit and feel focused on something other than the rush of school or pressures of grades.

And that pressure was building up for me. As nice as everyone was in trying to make me feel welcome, I had a much harder time trying to fit in with my studies. Getting into Briarcrest was a huge win for me, because I knew that it was the first of a lot of steps to get me to college, on to the pros, and most important, out of the ghetto.

But the going was rough. It was very difficult at first, and my biology teacher, Mrs. Beasley, was the first one who caught on that I did know the material. She noticed that I seemed to do okay answering questions she asked in class, but when it came to reading and answering questions on a test, I was stuck. She tried reading the test out loud to me, and when she found I could answer the questions that way, she realized that I wasn't slow at all—I just had never been in a caring classroom long enough to learn how to study and test effectively.

As soon as that became clear, all the teachers and administrators snapped into action to help figure out the best way to help me catch up and strengthen my study skills. The biggest challenge for me wasn't learning the material—it was having to break old habits and get away from comfortable behaviors that I had slipped into over the past ten years. I couldn't coast anymore; I had to really put my brain to work! I had to learn a whole new way of thinking and living—and I just needed people around me who cared enough to show me how to do that.

Sometimes I was pulled out of class to do extra work, and sometimes the teacher would stay after class and do some one-on-one tutoring with me. And the more I learned, the more I wanted to learn. Some of my teachers told me later that I was one of the most eager students they'd ever had. I looked forward to school and was excited to study because it was such a thrill for me to be learning so much so quickly.

The hardest part at first was not grasping the material; it was grasping the idea that the teachers actually cared about my progress. Except for one year in Ms. Logan's class and at Ida B. Wells, I had never known that kind of concern. Everyone seemed to care about improving my study skills so I could improve my grades, and I felt like I was starting to move forward.

I also realized that I couldn't get away with my old standby trick from the public schools anymore: copying directly from the textbook. If we had an assignment, I would open up the book and just write down a page or two, exactly as it appeared in the book. I figured that the right answer had to be on the page somewhere. The first time I did it in public school and got back a B on the assignment, I knew that there was no way the teacher was even looking at what I was doing because otherwise it would have been obvious that I'd taken the easy way out. But at Briarcrest I realized I was going to have to work for every grade I earned—and the crazy thing was, I was happy to do it.

Ms. Linda Toombs, the guidance counselor in charge of

scheduling, worked closely with me each semester to help me arrange a schedule that would meet all of the requirements, and also allow me to take advantage of the ESS program in a way that was better suited for my needs. She was a huge help to me in understanding what classes I needed to take and then making sure that I would have someone help me learn the study skills to succeed in them. Ms. Macki Lavender was my ESS teacher all three years, and she did wonders in helping me crack the code on how to learn.

Everyone has a different way of learning, and my teachers began to try out different styles to find mine. We quickly realized that the more I was involved with the material—like acting it out or reading it out loud or talking through it—the better I did. Things were sticking and I was able to build on them with new material. It was a huge rush.

Ms. Lavender would help me work on my assignments, especially for my English classes, as I learned how to do things like write research papers, which was totally foreign to me. We did a lot of memorization work my senior year, too. Students were supposed to learn important passages from famous books and recite them in front of the class. I was so excited when I learned mine by heart that the second I saw my English teacher, I begged to say my piece. It didn't matter that we were in the middle of the lunch line; I just rattled the whole thing off because I was so proud of what I'd accomplished.

I wasn't always so enthusiastic about memory work, though. In fact, I remember how happy I was when I finished writing my first paper—and then Ms. Lavender told me I needed to cite it.

I panicked. "I have to recite it? I can't learn this whole thing by memory!"

Ms. Lavender explained that citing the paper just meant that

I have to record where I got the information. That made me laugh hard because I was so relieved, but it also made me realize that I was starting to turn a corner in my confidence.

I think that a lot of times students who come from rough backgrounds struggle to learn because they are afraid to embarrass themselves by asking questions about what they don't understand. Ms. Lavender did a good job of making my learning time with her very relaxed, which meant that it felt like a safe place to ask questions. I didn't have to be afraid that she would be annoyed or frustrated or think I was dumb. She made me feel comfortable so that I could feel confident enough to ask for explanations on what I was still trying to learn. That was something I had never done before and I think it was a huge obstacle in my schoolwork.

AS MY STUDY PLAN DEVELOPED and my performance in class improved, I was able to bring my grades up to the point that the principal approved me to play the very end of the basketball season that first year at Briarcrest. I can't tell you what a huge victory that was for me to know that my hard work in the classroom was going to pay off for me on the court. I spent plenty of time on the bleachers that winter, watching the team practice and wanting so badly to be down there playing with them. That was my motivator. If I ever found I was thinking about giving up, I would go down to the gym and watch the team. That helped remind me why I was going through all the extra work. It would be worth it to get a shot to play ball, and maybe get noticed by a junior college scout.

I ran track that spring after basketball ended, and surprised everyone with my speed in the 40-meter dash. I also tried discus-throwing because a coach suggested it. I'd never even heard of such a thing, but he seemed to think I might be good at it. So I took the discus, watched a couple of other people take their turns to study their stance—and then I threw. Apparently, I did pretty well because my coach started laughing like a maniac when they measured where it hit, and after that discus became part of my training and competition list for the rest of my high school track career. (In fact, in 2005, I was the state runner-up in discus at the Tennessee high school track and field finals.)

By the time the summer before my junior year rolled around, I was ready for football to start. The stadium was at the new campus and that was where we met to kick off the football season.

Like a lot of high schools, Briarcrest had a group of kids who played a sport every season. They would go from football to basketball to track or soccer or whatever else was available. What was so great about Briarcrest, though, was that most of the guys didn't act like the typical high school jock-jerks you see in teen movies. They were actually great people who made me feel welcome and helped look out for me. I had gotten to know some guys a lot better with basketball and track, but I started to make some solid friendships once football practice started that summer.

Summer also marked the beginning of another important change in my life. While my teachers were working on my academic needs, I was still left with the very basic problem of where to live. I had decided I couldn't keep living with Tony and Steve all the time because I felt like I'd worn out my welcome with other members of the family. But I didn't really have an alternative. That was when a couple of wonderful families stepped up to help me. There was Matt Saunders, who was one of the coaches for the football team. He let me stay at his home a few times. There was the Sparks family, whose son Justin was on the team with me. They had an absolutely enormous house very close to

Briarcrest's new campus. They invited me to stay with them a lot, and it was my first real look into the side of Memphis I'd never known: the lives of wealthy white people. But amazingly, with the Sparks family as with just about everyone else at Briarcrest, our racial difference was not even an issue.

The family that did the most for me during that time, though, was the Franklins. Quinterio Franklin was on the football team, and I felt like I had more in common with him than pretty much anyone else at the school. He was black and his family was not very well-off financially and, to be honest, that just felt more comfortable to me. The Franklins lived about thirty miles south of Memphis, so it was a long ride to school each morning and a long drive back in the evenings—especially after games. But they didn't seem to mind having an extra person crammed into their small trailer house. I'm sure I made things feel even smaller, but it was so nice to be with a family that made me feel at home. They let me keep some clothes there, and they were generous with their food. They had nothing to gain by taking me in; they didn't do it for any reason other than that they had big hearts and they knew I needed a place to go.

At that point, one of the challenges I was facing was knowing that if I went back to Alabama Plaza, where my mother was living, or if I went back to my favorite barbershop for a straight-razor shave, which helps me avoid painful razor bumps, I was now an outsider.

My mother was fine with the fact that I was going to a different school, but she didn't really care that it was more demanding and made me responsible for my work in a totally new way, and she didn't even seem that interested in what I was achieving athletically. If Tony picked her up before a game or a meet, she would go to cheer me on. But otherwise, she simply didn't get involved. It felt like she didn't actually have any interest in what I was doing or even where I was living.

I felt like an outsider around a lot of other people, too. I was now going to a fancy private school on the other side of town. Some people wanted to tease me about it and other people saw it as a kind of betrayal—like I wasn't being true to who I was or where I came from. I just didn't have much of a place in the old neighborhood. So I owe a lot to the Saunders family and the Sparks family, but especially the Franklin family for opening up their homes to me and letting me stay there for as long as I needed. They will always have a special place in my heart for the amazing kindness that they showed me. I was on scholarship and had enough clothes, so all I really needed was food and a place to sleep, but I know that's still a lot to ask. If I was an inconvenience, no one showed it.

By my senior year, the scouts had started to notice me and the college coaches had started coming to see me play. So it was pretty clear that my grades mattered more than ever. And more than ever, folks stepped up to help me achieve my dream. Now, it wasn't just about helping me earn my high school diploma; it was about helping me reach the next level. At 6:30 every morning— an hour before school started—I would take an extra class of foundational study skills to help me make up for the gaps in my earlier education, and sometimes I would review my homework and lessons to make sure that I was staying on task and learning the material at the rate I needed to. This helped give me the learning tools and the confidence to take on the rest of my regular schedule.

But the teachers weren't just interested in helping to make me NCAA eligible. I could tell that they were teaching me because they wanted me to learn and because they knew I could. It was amazing to have that kind of support.

I've never struggled with the question of whether I could succeed; I only struggled with how. I was going to find a way, one way or another. I wasn't sure of the exact path, but I knew I wasn't going to give up until I'd achieved a better life for myself. The way that teachers and families at Briarcrest rallied around me finally showed me the missing piece in the puzzle. It was a busy and pretty crazy time, with a lot of moving pieces and a lot of complications.

And one family stepped up to the line to help me steer through it all.

CHAPTER TWELVE

Finding a Family

My transition into life at Briarcrest was a rewarding one, but it was still a transition. I was still stuck with the lack of a normal family and though several wonderful ones stepped up and let me stay in their homes, I knew that those arrangements couldn't be permanent.

So even as I stayed with the Franklins and Sparks and Saunders, I worried about where I could stay for good. I don't think that anyone really understood the degree to which I had nowhere else to go back to. I didn't talk about it much. I'm sure if anyone had known I was homeless, they would have called Child Protective Services believing they were acting in my best interest, and I would have found myself right back in foster care. That was the last thing I wanted, so I kept quiet.

I just tried to do my best, was respectful of the house where I was staying, and presented the best face that I could. The best way I knew how was to stay clean-shaven and always—always—ironed my clothes. I still do. It doesn't matter if it was a shirt for school or basketball practice, I never wanted to look sloppy, so I did laundry regularly and ironed out every last wrinkle. That was one thing I had noticed: The people at Briarcrest always looked neat. If I was going to be a part of their world, I was going to make sure I was neat, too. Over the past few years, I had used my money from selling newspapers to buy myself clothes and I had enough that still fit me, so I just did my best to take care of what I owned and prayed that they wouldn't wear out before I outgrew them.

In the meantime, strange things were happening at school.

One of the biggest differences between Briarcrest and all the other schools I'd attended was that lunch wasn't free. In my public schools I always made sure I was in school at lunchtime even if we didn't go to any classes during the day—at least I was guaranteed one meal a day. But at Briarcrest, everyone had to pay or pack. Free lunch wasn't an option; my scholarship just covered tuition. So suddenly I found out that the one meal a day I always knew I could count on was gone.

Again, it was a situation where if I had told anyone, I know they would have immediately helped me out. But I didn't, and I guess it just didn't occur to anyone that two or three dollars a day for lunch was more than I could afford. It was one thing to bum a bed on the sofa or some food at dinnertime. It was a totally different thing to ask for money for lunch. So I just did my best to make do, having a snack if someone offered me something in the lunchroom and hoarding food whenever I could to always have a little stash I could go to.

But suddenly I discovered that I had a lunch account. I can't remember who told me, specifically, but I just know that one day I was told that I could just get whatever I needed in the lunch line and it would be covered. The feeling of relief that day was huge. I was starting to see God at work around me; I had a need, it was met. That's pretty powerful.

Later I would find out it was Sean Tuohy who was my cafeteria sponsor. I should have guessed it was him because he seemed especially interested in getting to know me. He was a volunteer coach for the basketball team, so I had gotten a chance to talk with him a little bit at the end of the season my sophomore year, when I first started to play. He did a lot with the track team then because his daughter, Collins, was on the team.

I had noticed him before I even started playing basketball, when I would sit in the bleachers to watch practice and remind myself of why I was working as hard as I was. He seemed like a smart coach and a nice guy. He must have noticed me, too, because he came over and talked to me one day. It wasn't much—just a little introduction—but then I saw him again when I started playing ball and when track started up; it was nice to feel like I had a connection to one of the coaches. It would still be a long time before I would be a part of his family, though.

SCHOOL HOLIDAYS WERE SCARY TIMES FOR ME. Every other kid would be so excited about the break, talking about where their family was going on vacation or how late they were planning to sleep in. But I dreaded the times when the school would be closed. It was easy to catch a ride home with someone after practice, and then stay the night. But no school meant no practice, which also potentially meant no place to sleep. Like I said, if any one of the families I was staying with had realized that I really had nowhere to go, I know they would have welcomed me without a second thought. But I didn't volunteer the information. In truth, my mother was back on drugs and I was afraid to go back to my old neighborhood because I felt like it might swallow me up one day and never let me back out.

Thanksgiving break of my junior year was just one of those times. A big winter storm was moving in, with sleet and wind. That was okay, though, because I had decided that I would go to the gym at the old campus to shoot hoops. I bundled up the best I could in long pants and a sweatshirt, and set off. I felt responsible, like I was doing my homework for basketball. And I felt some pride and ownership of that space: It was my school, and since I was part of the team, it was my gym, too. I knew it would be warm there, and sheltered. It seemed to me like heading to the gym was a smart decision, given the situation. It never occurred to me that it might not be open.

I didn't even notice the silver BMW that drove past me that November morning; the part of town I was walking through is full of BMWs. It wasn't until the car turned around and pulled up to me that I realized Coach Tuohy was driving, and there was a very tiny, very loud lady sitting next to him. When they told me that the gym was closed, I agreed to let them take me to a bus stop.

A week or two later, once school was back in session, Coach Harrington talked to me after practice one day to tell me that one of the parents at school wanted to take me shopping for some new clothes. Would I be okay with that? I wasn't sure why anyone would want to go shopping with me, but I agreed. The next day Coach Tuohy's wife, Leigh Anne, loaded me up in her car and we headed to a big and tall men's shop I knew of on my end of town.

She still teases me about all the striped rugby shirts I picked out, and that scene made it into the movie. But what the film doesn't show is the hideous shirt covered in flowers and palm leaves that she pulled for me to try on. It looked like something an old man would wear on the beach in Hawaii. It was truly ugly! I passed on that. But I did end up with some shirts that, for maybe the first time, actually felt like they fit the way they were supposed to fit. I always felt like too-small clothes just made me look bigger, and as a teenager I was still very self-conscious about my size. But clothes that were loose felt like they might hide me a bit more instead of making me look like I was so huge I was about to rip out of them like the Incredible Hulk.

As I got to know the Tuohys, they invited me to come to their house after school, an invitation I ended up accepting pretty quickly. They lived just a couple of blocks from the old campus, so I already was familiar with the area, even though high school classes had moved to the new campus south of the city. Coach Tuohy would drive me over to their house after basketball practice sometimes, and I would stay for dinner (which was whatever they ordered in, since no one in the family liked to cook). Then he would drive me back to wherever I was sleeping at the time, usually stopping at a fast-food place somewhere along the way to order me something to tide me over until breakfast.

One evening after a track meet, when I didn't give Sean a clear answer as to where I would be staying that night, they invited me to stay the night on the sofa in the game room. And so the Tuohy family became part of my rotation. I would stay with them for a couple of nights, always trying to be sure I was a good guest by making a very neat bed with the sheets and blankets they offered, and folding them up neatly on the corner of the sofa in the morning.

The more time I spent with that family, the more I felt like I had found a home. It might have been a little bit of a crazy home with people who seemed always to be running in and out, between Collins's friends stopping by all the time and Sean and Leigh Anne's work schedules, but it was a comfortable kind of crazy.

To be a part of a community at Briarcrest, as well as starting to feel like part of a supportive family, made all the difference in the world for me, because I'd never been around people who were cheering me on. One of the most important things going on for me at that time was building relationships, because that was something that had been lacking in my life. Of course I had my biological family and I loved them fiercely, but as I mentioned, love was something we never discussed much in my family. We never, ever said those words to one another. And yes, while everyone around us, from social workers to foster families, could see that we all had a deep love for one another—and it is more important to show love than just to say it—a child still needs to hear those words, too.

It had been a challenge for me up to that point to feel real relationships with anyone outside of my immediate circle. I never developed relationships with other foster care kids because I knew we probably wouldn't be together long. After all, my view of the world was that if you had family bonds, you all got split up eventually. And with foster parents, it was hard for me to believe that they loved me even if they were kind and welcoming. They didn't birth me; they didn't hold me when I was little. They might come to love me like their own eventually, but it was hard to believe anyone could feel that way about me right off the bat.

But I felt like the Briarcrest community wanted me there, wanted to build relationships with me, wanted to make me feel welcomed into the school's family. And I started to feel like the Tuohys really wanted me there, too, and that they might really love me.

I didn't start out by staying there every night. It would just be a night or two at a time before I went somewhere else. But the Tuohys started asking questions. Leigh Anne isn't a lady who just lets things go. She asked about my family, and while I wasn't ready to open up, I did like how she was concerned about me. I liked that she wanted to know where I was going when I left their house, even if I didn't want to tell her. I liked that she and Sean noticed me. I didn't feel invisible when I was with them. I liked that Collins was down to earth, not snobby like so many other girls. I liked that S.J., their son, who was just seven at the time, treated me like a big brother when I was over there, just like I had treated my own big brothers, way back when we were all still together.

They didn't crowd me with emotion, but they also made sure I knew I was always welcome. They didn't treat me like I was fragile, or with curiosity like I was a strange creature they had to figure out before we could get close. They treated me just like they treated everyone else, and I think that helped me feel so at home there so quickly.

I also got the sense that they seemed to understand what I was trying to do, but that I just didn't have the tools—or even know what the tools were—that I needed to get there. I wasn't dumb and I wasn't lazy. I was lost and hurt and I wanted to work hard but hardly knew where to start because ambition just wasn't anything I'd ever really seen modeled in my life.

For me just to see how those families lived—all the Briar-crest families that took me in—what their neighborhoods were like, what the rules and expectations were in their homes, had a huge impact because I was able to understand what I'd suspected, that a life like mine in childhood wasn't normal and it wasn't okay. And I started to get a much clearer picture of what I was aiming for.

Because my dream wasn't about making the big bucks, it was about making a better life than what my brothers and sisters and foster siblings and I had all known. Those different families I stayed with all showed me that it was possible to feel safe from violence at night and that there actually are adults who work hard during the day and take care of their kids and encourage them to succeed in school and whatever their dreams are. And the Tuohys were the ones who were able to pour themselves into my life to help me make the most of the doors that I was trying to open.

That partnership was important for all the pieces to fall into place. I was trying to open doors and they were trying to show me the way through. It never would have worked if it had been one-sided: just me pushing but not knowing what to do with the opportunity; or them trying to guide me but me not being willing to do any of the work. There had to be a give and take.

The summer before I began my senior year of high school, the Tuohys invited me to live with them full-time. My mother didn't really care one way or the other that I was moving out, but I was thrilled. I had started staying there most of the time, but occasionally I still would stay at other homes, too. Having a place where I could say, "I'm going home" was exciting for me. They cleared out the loft room above S.J.'s bedroom. It had been his playroom, but I didn't mind if the pop-a-shot basketball game stayed, since he and I could (and have) played it for hours at a time. The room had high ceilings, which was nice for me to not feel like I might bump my head if I stood on my toes.

Leigh Anne drove me around to all the different homes where I'd stayed and I collected the clothes or shoes I had left there to always have something to wear for school. And when I carried everything upstairs to put it in the closet, I felt like I finally had a place in a normal home. Every night, Leigh Anne would tell the kids good night by saying, "I love you." She said it to me, too, and I started to believe she meant it.

Everything was so different from how it had been when I'd been placed with foster families. The Tuohys treated me like a member of the family—a real family—and not just as another mouth to feed or the reason for a monthly support check. I was building real relationships with the people around me; I wasn't just a special project to them. I was a kid who wanted to feel loved and supported and to know that my dreams and my future were just as important as anyone else's.

It didn't take long to adjust to life there. In no time, Collins and S.J. became as real a brother and sister to me as the ones I was related to by blood. I bonded with both of them quickly—and bonding between siblings can mean fighting, too. I would wake up early and be ready to leave for school by six o'clock. Collins, on the other hand, would roll out of bed ten minutes before first period was supposed to start. I love that she is not a high-maintenance girl who needs hours to get ready, but it would drive me crazy. Just like when I had AAU basketball practice as a kid and would always be the first one to practice, I wanted to be the first one to school. That was where I was supposed to be and it was my responsibility to be there on time. Even on mornings when I didn't have my extra class before school started, I wanted to get there early, and if she and I were driving together, I would start to get nervous and impatient, pacing back and forth and calling upstairs every two minutes, "COME ON!!!" Days we didn't drive together, she would often meet me in the hallway to hand me my helmet or cleats or something I had forgotten in my rush to get out the door.

The same thing would happen on Sunday mornings. The Tuohys never told me I had to go to church with them, but if I was staying with them and they were my family, I felt I needed to go with them. I'd be the first one with my shirt and tie on, sitting downstairs on the sofa and looking at my watch constantly. I liked church. I wanted to be there on time. I didn't want to come in late because, let's be honest, there's no way someone like me can slip down the aisle into an empty spot in the pew totally unnoticed.

It was those little quirks in our relationship that let me know we were really a family. I could get frustrated or annoyed at someone, and they could get frustrated or annoyed with me. We didn't have to worry about being polite to one another all the time because I wasn't a guest. It was my house, too. They used to tease me as we'd drive to church because I would point out various corners where I used to sell papers, including the one where I made the most money, until a Walmart was opened just a block or so away and it took away my business. After a few weeks of that, whenever we'd all be in the car driving somewhere, someone would point to a random place on the street and say, "Did you sell papers there, Michael?" (Sometimes, they'll even do it in a totally different city, and it always makes me laugh.) I loved the joking because it meant that I was as real a part of the life of that family as anyone else. It was wonderful.

There was just one condition for living with the Tuohys, and this had been made clear to me since I first started relying on them: They wanted to make sure I was going to keep a relationship with my birth family. At no point did they want there to be any kind of a feeling like they had taken me away from my mother, or kept me from her and made me cut all ties. I was nervous about those visits to see my mother at first. Sean and Leigh Anne didn't push me to tell them why, but it was the same fear I'd had ever since I started living with Tony. I felt like I was fighting for every inch of distance I got between me and the old neighborhood and the thought of going back seemed like it was dangerous because it might pull me back into old habits, old friendships, and old ways of thinking and acting. I didn't love my brothers or mother any less, but I felt like keeping a safe distance from the 'hood, at that point, was an act of survival.

But I went. Every other week or so I drove over to that side of town in Sean's Ford F-150 truck and I saw whichever of my brothers was around; usually it was Marcus or Carlos. I visited Craig whenever I could. I saw my mother, and it hurt so badly because I hated to see what drugs had done to her life. She was worn out, broken, and just a shell of herself. The loving, happy woman I remembered from when she was clean during my childhood didn't seem to be there, deep down in her soul anymore.

Eventually, Sean offered her a job at one of the Taco Bells that he owned near her home so that she would have a steady job that might help her stay clean. It was a good arrangement for about a week, but then she started not showing up for work or showing up on the wrong days. She kept at it, showing up occasionally, but at least she was still showing up. I wanted to know she was trying and I was glad Sean cared, too.

Sean and Leigh Anne wanted to make sure that my mother was a part of my football life as well. And that was a part of my life that was growing and taking off in ways that surprised even me.

CHAPTER THIRTEEN

Finding Football

As I mentioned earlier, basketball was my first love. From the time I watched that Phoenix-Bulls game when I was seven, I was obsessed with it. Football would be my favorite sport during football season, but when that was over, I'd go back to basketball. That was where I saw myself when I pictured my future—on the basketball court, the scariest thing to ever block a shot but also totally graceful as I flew through the air taking the ball to the basket. And it wasn't a crazy dream, either. I was really good at basketball, and a whole lot quicker and more skilled than anyone expected out of someone my size.

I had made enough progress academically in my first few months at Briarcrest that I was eligible to play the last couple of games of the basketball season. First, I played the last five that the JV had scheduled, but, unfortunately, there wasn't a jersey that fit me. I ended up playing in an old practice T-shirt with the school's name across the front and the number written on the back in permanent marker. It wasn't exactly the most sophisticated-looking uniform, but it worked. The varsity season was a little bit longer, and I was able to play the last six games of their season; but by that point, someone had made me a better team shirt with the numbers actually ironed on instead of drawn.

We did very well the next two years and actually ended up as the runners-up to the state Division II title my senior season, and my high school stats were an average of 22 points per game and 10 rebounds; but sometimes I had a frustrating time on the court, since I was still having the same issues with fouling that had always haunted me when I played. The refs seemed to love to blow the whistle at me for fouling the other team even though I actually wasn't doing it very much at all. I just had so much body, being well over six feet and about three hundred pounds at the time, that it didn't seem like a fair match-up for whoever I was covering, or maybe they just weren't used to watching someone that big on the court and couldn't see around me all the time to recognize that I really wasn't committing any more fouls than anyone else. It finally got to the point that I could hardly step out on the court without the ref blowing his whistle at me. I was so frustrated that I didn't know what to do—it felt like the refs were competing to see who could call more fouls on me each game. The Briarcrest coaches, and even the fans, were getting fed up with it, too. They could all see that I wasn't being overly physical or aggressive with anyone, but the refs seemed to think I was an easy target to make calls against.

The situation finally got resolved when Leigh Anne came marching into the gym before a game one day carrying a video camera. She introduced herself to the referees, pointed me out to them as her son, and let them know that there had been some problems about a lot of unfair fouls being called against me in the past. She told the ref that she would be personally record-ing the game, and if there were any blatant calls against me that clearly were not accurate, she would be sending the tape to the Tennessee Secondary School Athletic Association to make sure that the ref never called another game for Briarcrest. That did the trick. Any foul called after that was one I deserved.

The style of basketball they played there was totally different not just from the street-ball rules I had grown up with, but also from the way we played in the city schools. The coaching style was different, too. Tony had been excited about Briarcrest as an option when he found out their new coach was a well-respected high school coach named John Harrington, but for me, the new way of doing things made me back off of basketball a little bit. I stayed with it and played varsity basketball my junior and senior years— but my focus started to shift from the court to the gridiron.

Everyone seemed to think that the football field was the place for me, but I wasn't so sure at first. I loved the game, but as I started practicing for the season my junior year, I discovered that I didn't love to play it in such a structured way. At Briarcrest, the game was more mental, while at Westwood, Manassas, and the empty lots around Hurt Village, the game was much more physical. With Coach Hugh Freeze at Briarcrest, we didn't spend nearly as much time doing weight training as I had with Coach Johnson at Westwood. At first I was a little frustrated, but then I realized that most of my new teammates weren't going to college to play sports. If they were given an opportunity to play in college, they'd take it, but these were pretty much all kids who were going to college for academics. Their scholarships were going to be for their grades more than for their sports statistics. A guy like me, for whom athletics was going to be my ticket to school, who would have to fight to get the grades to even be considered by a college—I was a new type of player, and I don't think the coaches at Briarcrest really knew just what to do with me at first.

One thing I definitely understood, though, was how the game worked. In the movie *The Blind Side*, you see S.J. teaching me different plays using ketchup bottles and spices. I know stuff like that makes for a good story on screen, but in reality, I already knew the game of football inside and out. Like I said before, I didn't just watch it as a kid—I studied it, learning the plays and what each position did. When I was struggling with homework at school, studying sports was a subject where I could have been an honors student. I didn't just learn the rules, but I studied every play and every position, trying to understand strategy and technique. Yeah, it might have taken a little while for me to get used to a new way of playing at Briarcrest, but it wasn't because I didn't know what was going on; it was because understanding the how and whys of something is a lot different from doing it in real life.

Learning to play with a lot of structure and a coach who was demanding in a different kind of way was very important, though. What I came to realize is that I would have to be able to do that in order to get to college and to survive there. You can be the best player in the world, but if you are un-coachable because of your attitude, you'll never get anywhere. Talent will only take you so far. You've also got to be willing to work with your team and respect your coach.

In my case, I knew I was good, but I also knew I had a lot more to learn about putting everything I understood about the game into my body and making it totally natural when I played. I also was frustrated a lot because we couldn't seem to find the right place for me on the team. Everyone said I was a natural-born football player, but no one seemed sure where to play me.

We had to try a bunch of different positions on the defensive line until we finally found the best fit. It was easy to see that right or left tackle was a good place for me, and I could play either one, but once Coach Freeze put me in at left tackle, everything changed. I started to love the game in a way I never knew I could before because I wasn't just playing a game. I had a responsibility, a job. I was protecting the quarterback, but I also had to watch everyone else in the lineup and guess as to how the charge to the line would play out. I think that after quarterback, of course, left tackle is the biggest intellectual challenge in the entire game.

Some people may think after watching the movie that I'm a dumb kid who just blocks well, but I'd like to see any of them try to stand in as left tackle for even one play, and see how effective they are at reading the defensive line. This isn't a position for dummies. I could tell that right away, and after each game, my brain felt almost as sweaty as my body. It was a workout for my mind, and I hit the showers feeling like I'd just finished reading some huge book, which was a great feeling.

Just like in basketball, though, I kept running into challenges with pointless calls by some refs. The rules required that your jersey had to stay tucked into your pants, but mine was never long enough, so it would always come out during games, no matter how many times I kept tucking it in. The rules also were very specific, for some reason, about the bottom of the shirt having a finished seam. Once Leigh Anne saw that this was an ongoing problem for me and that the refs seemed to be hung up on calling me out for this, she took my jerseys to a professional seamstress who sews curtains and other things for her decorating business. They got some jersey fabric and added about five or six inches onto the bottom of all of my football shirts and made sure that the edge was perfectly sewn in a professional seam. It was great! I could tuck my jersey into my football pants and not worry about it. I didn't have to constantly check to make sure all the edges were tucked back in between every single block, or to make sure that the bottom didn't sneak out when I got into position to run the next play.

At first, all of the excitement over my skills on the field seemed a little crazy. I knew I had been blessed with athletic talent, but I still thought of myself as a basketball player who just happened to be good at football, too. My stats started to climb, and I soon realized what a lot of college coaches were seeing: I was just about the toughest left tackle around. During my two years of varsity football at Briarcrest, I didn't allow a single sack.

By the time recruiting visits started up my senior year, I was totally overwhelmed by the attention. I kept finding my name in the national rankings for high school recruits—ranking systems and top ten lists I didn't even know existed. Suddenly, it seemed like every college around was beating on my door to get me to go there, when just a few years before it had been a bit of a fight just to get into high school.

It was a challenge, meeting all of those important coaches. I've always been shy, but I was especially nervous about sitting down and having a conversation with them. I was nervous about traveling overnight to visit the schools. All those old doubts about trusting people began to sneak back in. What would they think of me? They all knew my background—would they decide I'm not the kind of person they want on their team? And what about my manners? The last thing I wanted was to come off as ignorant.

That was a big issue in the Tuohy house. Leigh Anne threw herself into the task of making sure I knew my way around a fancy dinner table and that I had a good sense of what certain restaurant dishes were. We would go out to different fancy restaurants in town and we would order pretty much everything on the menu. She'd explain to me a little about each dish, and I'd try to get an idea of what it tasted like and how to handle it on my plate. Her goal wasn't to "fix" me, as if not knowing those things somehow made me broken. Not at all. She just wanted to make sure that I would feel comfortable in any situation, and I am glad that she did. Now I can walk into any interview, any nice restaurant, any sporting event, and feel confident about how I come across.

It might sound like a silly thing to worry about with football coaches coming to town. A coach doesn't care if you know the difference between the different forks in a place setting or if your tie comes from Walmart or Brooks Brothers. They really don't. It's not about impressing them with fashion or flashy jewelry or a nice house—I guarantee you that any Division I coach is probably richer than 99 percent of the kids he recruits. They aren't there to be impressed by anything about you except the fact that you are a good athlete and a reliable player.

But I came to understand that first impressions do matter, and as a college athlete, you are ultimately a representative of your team, your coach, your program, and your school. The same is true wherever you go in life, whatever your job may be. There is a right way and a wrong way to act in different settings. It is so important to have a basic working understanding of etiquette. You can't act the same way in a McDonald's as you would in a fine dining restaurant. You can't talk to a coach the same way you would talk to your friends. It is so important to have a sense of the situation and what kind of behavior it requires. It's not a matter of snobbery; it's a matter of understanding how the world works and showing your smarts by picking up on the difference of each setting.

It is a lesson I am very, very grateful for because it is definitely something I had never even considered when I was living in my old neighborhood, and it makes a big difference—fair or not—in how other people see you. It is the same reason that I always care about ironing my clothes and taking care of my appearance. I want to give the impression of being put-together and respectable. Commentator Chris Collinsworth made a remark to Bob Costas when they were doing the commentary for a Ravens game one time that when you first met me you'd think I had just left the local country club. I appreciated that because it meant that I came across as polite and intelligent.

When I sat down with each of those college coaches or went on those recruiting visits, I wanted to make sure that they knew what they would be getting in me: a guy who would play his heart out and give every ounce of effort to the game, but also someone who would represent the program well. After all, this wasn't just a game to me. This was my life's goal of achieving something better turning into reality.

In the end, after visits to several schools and meetings with a lot of coaches, I picked the University of Mississippi. Tennessee and Oklahoma were both schools I liked a lot, but in the end, I was most comfortable about being closest to the community I'd become a part of. Just like I had wanted to go wherever Steve went to high school, I wanted to be near wherever Collins went to college, close enough to see S.J.'s baseball games, close enough for Leigh Anne and Sean to come to my football games. I had been separated once before from the family I loved. Now I finally was part of a stable family, and had good mentors, good support, and a lot of people who believed in me. I wasn't about to give all of that up to start over again somewhere else.

MY SENIOR YEAR, my mother started trying to make it to a lot of my Briarcrest games, sometimes bringing one of my brothers or

Craig along, too. Before Senior Night for football, Leigh Anne gave her money to pick out a nice church dress to wear as the seniors were escorted out on the field by their parents. Tony was driving my mother over and they were running late. The announcer had gotten to just before the Os and they still weren't there, so Sean and Leigh Anne brought me back in line to the Ts, where they were waiting to walk out with Collins. Just before they called us up, I spotted my mother running across the track in a gold dress. She was out of breath as she took my arm, but she made it and I walked out on the field with her on one side and the Tuohy family on the other.

That was me, my life. My past and my future were there on each side of me as we walked into the middle of the football field. I had come from one family and been welcomed into another— many others, including the Hendersons, the Franklins, the Tuohys, and the Briarcrest family at large. I smiled as I looked up at the crowd in the bleachers who were cheering for me because I knew I was home.

CHAPTER FOURTEEN

Miss Sue

As my senior year got under way in the fall of 2004, and I was meeting with all those coaches to decide on which college to attend, I was so excited about my future. I had reached my full height of six feet four, and my weight matched that so I wasn't just big or just tall and I looked like a man instead of a boy inside the body of a football player. But football alone wasn't going to get me to college, and it certainly wasn't going to help me graduate. My body finally may have slowed down growing, but my mind still was racing at a hundred miles an hour, hungry for whatever subject I was studying. That was where Miss Sue came in.

I can't talk enough about the time and work Miss Sue put into helping me. She is retired now, but she deserves to be in the Hall of Fame. She was such a hugely important part of my success both in high school and in college because she was the one who really gave me the confidence to know that I *could* learn, which is the first step in beating the odds.

Sue Mitchell was an Ole Miss grad and a high school English teacher who had been teaching in the Memphis schools since long before I was even born, so she knew what she was doing and she knew how different people study. She was the perfect person to help me tackle my classes.

As one of the most important parts of my support structure, Miss Sue shared my short-term and longer-term vision for myself. My goals were to 1) graduate high school, 2) qualify to play NCAA football, 3) go to college, and 4) play in the NFL. Looking at me on paper with my still-too-low GPA, those goals must have seemed impossible. But Miss Sue didn't judge me based on my transcripts and she didn't make assumptions based on my past. She looked at me as a person, as someone who was determined to do whatever it took to succeed, and she believed in me—truly believed in me— from day one. She didn't treat me in a patronizing way, like I was some little kid who needed applause or a crazy person with impossible dreams. She encouraged me and cheered me on, but she also kicked me in the butt and made me buckle down when that was what I needed, too. And I responded to that because I knew that she wasn't doing it for show. She believed that I had it in me to do what I wanted to do because I'd already come so much further than anyone would have ever expected me to.

ONCE I MOVED in with the Tuohys permanently, Sean and Leigh Anne decided to look around for a tutor to work with me in the evenings to help me get my grades up to where they needed to be for college. Miss Sue was the person who stepped up and started coming over to the house, five nights a week for four hours at a time. Since I had sports practice after school, we usually didn't get started on my homework until after six, and many nights we'd work until after ten. Sunday through Thursday (since I had games on Friday nights), she would sit down at the big dining room table with me and we would tackle my class assignments one by one.

I would read things on my own; we would read things out loud together; she would make me take notes on whatever we discussed and then encourage me to review them before going into class the next day. She also knew I was good at memorization, I guess because of having to remember the playbook in football, so we did a lot of memorization work to help me get the material in my head and then convert it into my own words to make that knowledge my own.

I don't know how many hours she spent going over things until I really got them. I wasn't just interested in learning for a test and moving on. I needed to know that I could learn whatever was necessary to succeed. Sometimes it took a while, but she never lost her patience. Well, she probably did lose her patience, but she never showed it.

The whole family got into that—especially Sean. He loves poetry and jumped at the chance to talk about it. Collins made sure her schedule matched with some of my classes so that we were able to study together, too. Everyone around me was pitching in to help me reach a potential I never knew I had. I mean, I never doubted that I could do whatever I set my mind to, but I had no idea that I could accomplish so much academically. But as we made parallels to my own life, sports, and other things that were more real to me than just the words on the page, all kinds of connections started to click. It was like a whole new world was opening up and I began to understand and appreciate science and literature as more than just subjects in school.

What is most amazing to me is that Miss Sue did it all for free. Where I came from, there was always a "You gotta get paid" mentality, but Miss Sue wasn't interested in teaching me—or anyone—for money. I mean, of course she had worked as a teacher professionally and got a paycheck for it, but it was clear to me from the beginning that she was someone who knows the reason God put her on this earth, and it is to teach people who need some extra help. No one would put in that kind of time and effort and work with that much passion if they were only doing it to get something material out of it. The patience she had with me as I worked through problems and assignments, and the excitement she had whenever I got them right, were real and came from a place inside that was concerned first and foremost with my achievement.

I have to admit, though, that it was tough at first for me to accept her help. I mean, I'd been relying on myself for so long that it was kind of scary to say to someone else, "Okay, I need you. I'm going to let you show me how this works." I'd had people looking out for me before, but never in quite the same way that Miss Sue did. She wasn't just teaching me skills, she was building my sense of confidence in my own abilities. She wasn't just helping me get through each day, she was working to help me meet my long-term life goals.

My last semester in high school, I made the honor roll, which remains one of the proudest accomplishments of my life. In order to attain the NCAA's GPA requirements, though, I needed to do some extra work to make up for my earlier years in high school before I got to Briarcrest and while I was still adjusting to a more rigid academic schedule.

Instead of jumping into summer vacation like so many of my friends, I began work with a series of online courses offered through Brigham Young University that were approved by the NCAA for core course requirements for athletes trying to improve their GPAs. The grades earned there can be used to replace older, failing grades on the transcript, and it was an exciting series of courses for me. Subjects covered a wide range, including foreign languages, math, social studies, business, and English. It was a wonderful program for kids like me to go back and redo some of the courses we didn't get right the first time.

Now that I was so much more confident in my ability to study, I gobbled up those courses, studying authors and historic figures, writing reports on poems and novels. Each time I finished one and got my grades back, I felt like I was erasing a failure from my past. Just because I didn't have someone to show me how to learn effectively when I was fifteen didn't mean I had to lose out on a chance for college now.

I was very fortunate to have such a strong support system of people who were really concerned with helping me catch up. If I had known how much work it was going to take to get my grades up, I would have been in the books more when I was younger. It was my freshman year, when I was still in the public schools and still cutting class a lot to hang out, that caused the problems. I am just grateful that I had the opportunity to make up for some of my earlier mistakes and poor decisions because I know that most kids in my situation don't get that second chance.

And, of course, Miss Sue was cheering me on the whole way. By the time I had brought my high school GPA up to the standard, I was excited about starting college in a way I never thought I would be. I wasn't just ready to play football; I was ready to start working on my degree.

Miss Sue, in the meantime, had applied for a tutoring job with the university and was offered the position! That fall, it wasn't just Collins and I who were moving to Oxford; Miss Sue moved there, too—something she said she'd been wanting to do since she'd graduated and left years before.

Her new job involved working with a number of athletes, including a number of my teammates, and everyone else loved her as much as I did. She really cared about us. We weren't just a job for her. She was excited for us and cared about how we did in the classroom and on the field, but she also cared about how our lives were going. She knew if someone broke up with his girlfriend or if someone was struggling with a bad family situation.

Miss Sue's investment in us was one we took seriously. We were all amazed by her patience and we felt her real concern for us. I know that her other student-athletes worked harder for her because they didn't want to let her down. No one likes to disappoint the people they love, and just the few hours we spent with her each week made it clear that she loved us all. (She loved me best, though!)

I KNOW THAT THERE WILL ALWAYS BE PEOPLE who think that the extra courses I took to help raise my high school GPA were a lame excuse for making up classes I failed the first time around. There are other people who will always be convinced that I am just a dumb football player who only graduated from Briarcrest because I had a lot of people helping to pull me along because they wanted to get me into college. All I can say in response to that is, look at my academic record while at Ole Miss. I wasn't just squeaking by with the minimum GPA—twice I made the dean's list. It's amazing how a life can turn around with some encouragement, some support, and someone willing to say, "I believe you CAN do what you've set your mind on doing."

Miss Sue is a huge part of my success because she helped me believe that I could do what so many people around me seemed to think I couldn't. She also goes to show that you don't have to just put a roof over a kid's head to make a difference in his life. There are other needs that have to be met, too, and she dedicated her own life to helping kids improve theirs.

CHAPTER FIFTEEN

Rebel with a Cause

When college coaches started showing up to recruit me, I couldn't believe that it was all starting to happen for me. So many things in my life had been such a disappointment that to suddenly find myself in a loving family that cared about my dreams and were committed to helping me reach them—it was almost too much. But as college began to become a reality for me, I still had to prove that I had the ability to do the schoolwork. I clearly had the drive, will, and discipline—I'd demonstrated that through my long hours of studying, homework, and extra coursework. But I still wanted to prove not only to myself but to everyone who had stepped up to help me that I had what it took to succeed.

One of the big fears coaches seemed to have was that I wouldn't be able to read and understand the playbook, because I had required so much extra work to help bring up my GPA. That kind of made me laugh because while I might have struggled with school and had to learn how to succeed in the classroom, I knew sports. I may not have spent much time poring over the various plays by name, but I understood strategy. I think that became clear the more the coaches watched me play.

When I finally decided to become an Ole Miss Rebel, it was like a huge weight had been lifted off my shoulders. I couldn't believe that in just a few short years I had gone from being a kid who was struggling to figure out how he would be able to get into a junior college to a kid who had a lot of major schools recruiting him and offering scholarships. And I really, really liked a couple of the schools I visited—I liked their coaches and their teams and how I felt when I was on their campus. It was such a tough decision.

By that point, I realized that God had blessed me and blessed my life with not just talent but people who were willing to help me develop that talent into something great. When it came down to the final couple of schools, I prayed about my choice a lot because there didn't seem to be a clear-cut sense of one being a good school and another being a bad school. I felt like wherever I chose to go would be a good decision and would be a place where I could keep growing as a player and as a person.

So when I made up my mind at last, I could finally breathe a little easier—it was like I'd been holding my breath for months. I didn't have a whole lot of time to enjoy the moment, though, since I still had to worry about my grades for graduation and eligibility. And I didn't get much of a summer break after graduating high school, either. All my friends from school were taking off on vacation and enjoying their last summer before college, but I was hitting the books for the last of those extra courses to help my GPA. And then almost as soon as that studying was over, it was time to pick up and move to Oxford, Mississippi, for football training.

It was a very busy summer for me, because there was one

other pretty major event that happened right after I graduated high school: I became a legal member of the Tuohy family. Leigh Anne and Sean had already assumed responsibility for me as guardians, which allowed them to sign my school permission slips and take me to medical appointments. This last step was the one that would make everything binding.

It kind of felt like a formality, as I'd been a part of the family for more than a year at that point. Since I was already over the age of eighteen and considered an adult by the state of Tennessee, Sean and Leigh Anne would be named as my "legal conservators." They explained to me that it means pretty much the exact same thing as "adoptive parents," but that the laws were just written in a way that took my age into account. Honestly, I didn't care what it was called. I was just happy that no one could argue that we weren't legally what we already knew was real: We were a family.

I wish I could say it was just an uneventful morning with a trip to the courthouse and then a nice brunch to celebrate. Unfortunately, I found my past and my future in conflict yet again.

My mother was going to be at the hearing to agree that she supported the decision to have the Tuohys listed as my next of kin and legal conservators, and we were supposed to pick her up on the way to court. Leigh Anne was driving (Sean was meeting us there), but when we pulled up to my mother's house in Alabama Plaza, she wasn't waiting for us. I ran inside to get her so we wouldn't be late, but a certain person answered her door who I knew was bad news. He was an old boyfriend of hers who she had broken up with before and who I had hoped was out of her life for good. But there he was and just the sight of him sucked all the joy out of what was otherwise a happy, joyful morning for me.

I stormed out to the car, and even though Leigh Anne wanted

to know what the matter was (she could tell from the look on my face that I was furious), I didn't say a word. My mother came running out a minute or two later and we all headed to the courthouse together. But I was haunted by seeing that man because it was just another reminder of the trap of bad decisions that she was stuck in. I had been surrounded by those kinds of bad cycles of behavior my entire childhood and finally felt like I had escaped. And yet on the very morning that I was legally breaking free from the 'hood, there was an in-my-face reminder of the kind of life that might have been mine.

It was very much a but-for-the-grace-of-God moment for me. I knew that I had escaped—but how many other kids were there who were just like me but would never get the chance I did? It was depressing to think about. I figured that I owed it to all those kids to do something great with the opportunities I'd been given.

The court hearing was quick—probably only about fifteen or twenty minutes, beginning to end. My mother was supportive of the whole thing and there wasn't a whole lot of emotion all around because it was just a matter of formalizing the way we'd all been living for the past year. After court, we all went out to brunch together to celebrate. Then we dropped my mother off and went back to the house—to *our* house.

I COULD NOT HAVE PICKED a better time to start at Ole Miss, if for no other reason than they had just opened the Indoor Practice Facility next to Vaught-Hemingway Stadium. I know that might sound silly, but if you've never practiced football in the mugginess of a Mississippi summer, you have no idea what a difference it makes to have a field that is shaded and has some climate control. There was also a brand-new weight room. Basically, it was a long way from the empty lots where we used to play football back in Hurt Village.

There wasn't any time for me to get used to things, though. I started as a true freshman instead of having a Red Shirt year to learn how it all worked. So all at once, I was doing two-a-day practices, learning a whole new playbook, and getting ready for college classes.

I decided to major in criminal justice. I was interested in a communications degree so that I could go into broadcasting someday, but I was also interested in the law and definitely had grown up around a lot of crime, so criminal justice was a good fit. It was also more practical because the classes worked better with my football schedule. My life suddenly was just a blur of workouts, classes, practices, homework, and then back to the dorm for a few hours of sleep before getting up to do it all again.

Dorm living wasn't as big an adjustment for me as for some students. I was used to living in a small space with a lot of other people, so that wasn't a problem for me at all. In fact, I loved it. I enjoyed being a part of a community, surrounded by friends and bonding together as a team. I would end up making some lifelong friends, including football teammates like Jamarca Sanford, who is the most loyal person I have ever met and is still one of my best friends. But the one thing that did take a lot of getting used to was meeting a ton of new teammates, coaching staff, and students around campus. Being a naturally shy person, this was the scariest thing of all.

It made such a difference for me, though, having a great support system around me—not just tutors like Miss Sue but a couple of high school friends and Collins and some of her friends. They made me feel like I belonged.

I also looked around and saw lots of kids who, like me, were the first people in their biological family to ever go to college. So many of them seemed really lost, since they didn't have anyone back home who understood how overwhelming that first semester can be, or to warn them about all the temptations that college life can bring. Many colleges now have programs in place to help students in that situation, but it's still tough when you can't call home and talk to someone who understands. I was lucky that all those hours around the Tuohys' dining room table after football practice taught me a lot about time management, which is so helpful when you have no parent around telling you to put down the PlayStation and finish your homework!

I AM PROUD TO SAY that thanks to my tutors, my family, and a lot of hard work, my freshman year was a success. Despite the people who worried that I wouldn't be able to deal with all of the pressures on my own, I had a pretty good season. My first game was on September 5 against the University of Memphis, playing right tackle. The next week, I started for the Rebels in our game against Vanderbilt, where we earned 400 total yards of offense (our highest of the season). When we played Alabama, we lost by three points, but the offensive line managed to not allow a single sack and I was awarded the Rebel Quarterback Club Trench Player of the Week Award. The very next game the offensive line didn't allow any sacks, either. All in all, it was a rough season for Ole Miss, but it was clear that we were growing as a team. I loved that Collins was on the sidelines with the cheerleaders, rooting us on, and that my family—the Tuohys as well as sometimes one of my brothers or my mother, which was a nice surprise—would come to the games and yell for me, too. At the end of the 2005 season, I was named to the First Team SEC All-Freshman, First

Team All-Quad Freshman Chrome Tackle Letius, and First Team Freshman All-America. It was a hard season, but exciting.

The next year, Steve Henderson started at Ole Miss, too. I had to laugh that I had followed him to Briarcrest and now he was following me to college. He played football his freshman year, and I was able to introduce him to all my friends on the team, which was something he had done our first year at Briarcrest. I liked that I was able to kind of look out for him and return the favor.

My sophomore year I was moved back to left tackle and started all twelve games. In our second week, after playing Missouri, I was named the Rebel Quarterback Club Trench Player of the Week and then won the award again later in the season after we played Alabama. I was named to the First Team All-SEC by the conference coaches. I also made the Chancellor's List (which is what the Dean's List for GPAs of 3.5 or above is called at Ole Miss) academically, which may have been my proudest moment of the entire year.

Junior year (the 2007 season) was a really good one for me. The offense racked up 534 yards, 229 rushing, against Mizzou. Against LSU, we totaled 466 yards, 201 rushing. My name was put forward as a possible winner of the Outland Trophy for the best interior lineman in the country, and I was named a Mid-Season All-American by *The Sporting News*. I didn't allow a single sack against Georgia or Northwestern, and I won the Rebel Quarterback Club Trench Award after the Florida, Arkansas, and LSU games. By the end of the season, I was named to the First Team All-SEC both by the coaches and the AP. CollegeFootball-News.com named me the #2 Offensive Lineman in the conference and #7 overall player in the conference. A number of other lists placed me as a top pick, too.

It was such an exciting time for me, but as the season wrapped up, I started getting a little impatient to go. Even though I had strong statistics that season, 2007 was not a good season overall for Ole Miss, and since the coach's job is always on the line when the team's record slips, I knew big changes were coming. Coach Ed Orgeron left in November and Houston Nutt was soon lined up to take over after resigning from the University of Arkansas. I respected Coach Nutt a lot, but I started to think that maybe I should ride the momentum of a good junior year and enter the draft.

On January 14, 2008, I announced my intentions to go pro and skip my senior year. I had waited so long and worked so hard to get to the pros, and now that I was eligible, I felt I should jump on the chance to enter the draft. But after I announced my decision, I started having second thoughts. The more I thought about it, the more I realized that my life wasn't just about football. The opportunity to go pro in a sport is absolutely amazing, but a football player's career usually isn't that long. I mean, think about what our bodies go through each week—that can wear you out quickly. In fact, I think the average professional career in the NFL is under five years. I plan to be in the league a lot longer than that, but you never know what injuries might end your playing days in a heartbeat. I realized that it was shortsighted of me to think I could just forget about finishing my degree in order to go play football. What was I going to do when it was time for me to hang up my cleats for good?

I decided that the only thing for me to do was to finish my education before entering the draft, so that's what I did. I had come too far to quit so close to having everything I'd ever worked for—a pro career *and* an education. I took my name out of the ring and committed to returning for my senior year. And I'm so glad I stuck around. Not only did I make the Chancellor's List again, but I also had a great senior football season under Coach Nutt. I got First Team All-American, First Team All-SEC, the Shug Jordan Award for the Southeast Offensive Lineman of the Year, the Colonel Earl "Red" Blaik Leadership-Scholarship Award, the 2008 Outland Trophy finalist, Conerly Trophy finalist, Lombardi Award semifinalist, and the SEC Jacobs Blocking Trophy. Plus, it was great getting to travel with my teammates, too, going all over the southeast and sometimes a little farther out to places like Texas for our Bowl game. I got to see more and do more than ever before.

All in all, it wasn't too bad for a kid no one had any hopes for. I had accomplished more than anyone else in the world (other than me) ever expected I could—and even I was surprised sometimes! After that final game in red and blue, I knew that the time was right for me to move on to my professional career, and I was so glad I hadn't stopped short. It's never been about football, but about becoming the best and fullest person I could be. And to think that I went from the kid with a GPA in the basement to going to college on a football scholarship—I was thankful and humbled by how far I'd come in just a few years. I knew that miracles really do happen.

CHAPTER SIXTEEN

The Draft

When a college athlete gets ready to go pro, one of the first and most important things he or she does is to pick an agent. Not only does your agent help you to make promotional deals and help you to expand your public image, but more important, they handle things like contract negotiations and draft visibility, and they help you in walking through the crazy world of professional sports. They are also trained in how to handle legal stuff and money management. In short, they are incredibly important.

There are a lot of very good agents out there, but, unfortunately, there are some not-so-good ones, too. If you've ever seen the movie *Jerry Maguire*, you know that there are some agents who really care about their clients and there are some who are all about the money—just as there are some athletes who only play for a check. I didn't want to be one of those players and I definitely didn't want one of those agents representing me, so I worried a little about which agent I should hire.

A number of my teammates were looking at going pro (a total

of nine Ole Miss players ended up signing with NFL teams that year), and lot of my friends decided to hire one particular agent who had a reputation for being a very ethical guy, who had several high-profile football players as his clients. This was an emotional decision for me because Sean and Leigh Anne had a longtime friend in Memphis, Jimmy Sexton, who is also a great, ethical agent with a lot of high-profile clients. (And conveniently, his office is located less than three miles from the Tuohys' house).

It was important to me that the decision be my own, though, and I was glad that my family understood that. In the end, I decided to sign with the agent many of my close friends chose. They were very positive people in my life and I wanted to stick with them. It was important to me that we all share something that would keep us connected and supported even as we went our separate ways after the draft.

Unfortunately, it soon became clear to me that even though the agency was really solid, it just wasn't the right match for me. In order to get ready for the NFL Combine in February, before the draft in the spring, agents send their players to workout facilities to do some intense preparation. I was sent to a facility in Texas run by Michael Johnson, the four-time Olympic gold medalist in sprinting. It was an amazing training center, and Johnson is obviously an incredibly talented athlete. The thing is, for my field position and body type, I didn't need to work on my sprints as much as I did my strength. I felt like I was being turned into a different kind of player.

However, I did pretty well at the NFL Scouting Combine. It was a great experience going to Lucas Oil Stadium, though being in Indianapolis in February made me really happy I had chosen a college in a much warmer and less snowy place.

The Combine is kind of like an audition for professional teams to check out the players who are eligible for the NFL draft. It's an invitation-only event, and all the athletes go through a number of tests so the coaches can see their skills, both physical and mental, in action. Included is the Wonderlic Test, a fifty-question test that you have to complete in twelve minutes to help the coaches look at your problem-solving skills. Athletes also have fifteen-minute interviews with interested teams, drug screening, and (as you can imagine) lots of physical tests. You get clocked for the 40-yard dash, 20-yard shuttle, 60-yard shuttle, and 3-cone drill. You're tested on how many 225-pound reps you can bench press, you're measured for both vertical jump and broad jump, and you're evaluated on drills that are specific to your position. Plus, you have your body measured and examined for injuries, and even your joint movement is evaluated. You get looked at and considered in every possible way so that the NFL teams can have the best sense of who you are, what you can do, and whether you have the potential to improve.

I did okay but knew I could have performed better than I did. I thought about it and prayed about the whole situation a lot, and I finally decided that maybe I needed to change agents after all. As much as I respected the agent I'd hired, and as much as I loved my friends from Ole Miss who were doing well with their training, I realized that I needed to be with someone who could better work with my style of play. I also felt I needed someone who knew me well enough to understand my unusual story. I was concerned that many coaches or scouts who'd read *The Blind Side* were forming opinions about me before they got to know me. The book presented me as a slow learner instead of someone who had just never had much solid instruction. I wanted to correct that view of things.

So I had the uncomfortable conversation with my agent and

then signed with Jimmy Sexton instead. I finally realized that his history with my family, as well as his location in Memphis and understanding of the city, were really valuable to me. I went to train in Nashville, at D1 Sports Training. There we concentrated on weight training and heavy lifting, and in less than a month I was already much stronger than I'd been. March 26, 2009, was Ole Miss's pro day, and I was on fire. This is basically a team's last chance to scope out the players they might want to draft, and the scouts all said they were excited about what they saw from me that day. I knew that I was at the top of the list for tackles for a lot of teams.

I did learn a lesson from that whole experience: If you make the wrong decision, it's never too late to make the right one.

Learning is part of growing up. It was important to me to make my own choice, and I'm blessed that my family loved me enough to support me in my first choice and then again support me when I realized I needed to make a change.

DRAFT DAY WAS LIKE A DREAM for me. In the weeks leading up to it, I was so nervous and so excited at the same time. After the Combine, most experts were saying I'd go in the top twenty; after Ole Miss's pro day, a lot of them were saying I'd be a top-ten pick. I was so ready to get to New York and see how it would all play out.

Then a few things happened that threatened to cloud the experience.

First, a few draft watchers speculated that I might not play with enough passion and drive now that I had been taken in by a stable, wealthy family. They said that might affect how hard I would work because there was no longer the motivation to get out of the ghetto. I just rolled my eyes at those remarks. I had been a part of the Tuohy family since before I started college, and it definitely hadn't watered down my work ethic then. It was ridiculous to say it might happen now.

I also started to hear some whispers that despite my work to show that it wasn't true, some coaches were still worried after reading *The Blind Side* that I was not smart enough to learn the playbook. That really upset me because I knew I would prove them wrong if they just gave me a chance. I wanted to show everyone my Chancellor's List letters or have them quiz me on the Ole Miss playbook, which I knew backward, forward, and upside down. Just because I'd had a rough time moving from one inner-city school to another didn't mean that I wasn't bright. I finally realized that the only way I could prove those fears wrong would be to get out there on the field when my time came, and show those coaches how quickly I could learn—and what they had missed out on.

The third thing that happened, though, stung most of all. A few weeks before draft day, ESPN draft analyst Todd McShay said that I had "character issues" and listed me as one of the three "riskiest picks" in the upcoming draft. I couldn't believe it. I didn't understand what he could have possibly meant. Just a few months earlier, in December, McShay wrote about me on ESPN .com, saying: "While he possesses the physical tools to warrant top-15 consideration, it will be interesting to see if he slips to the bottom half of the first round—or beyond—because of concerns regarding his work ethic, motor and overall toughness." I didn't understand how he could drop me from the top fifteen to being one of the "riskiest," and then to say that I had character issues. I had always worked so hard to live responsibly and train harder than anyone else.

In fact, I even looked up the definition of "character" after I heard McShay's remarks, because I thought that maybe I had the wrong idea about what it meant and I was not being fair to him by being offended by what he said. But everything I read about character just confirmed what I felt: The comments were totally off base and completely unexplainable.

Thankfully, Coach Nutt was just as confused by McShay's comments as I was. He talked to the Memphis *Commercial Appeal* about me, saying: "I've had him for a year and there isn't a better person than Michael. He never was belligerent, always 'Yes-sir, no-sir,' worked hard in the weight room, voted captain and he played great all season long." It made me feel so much better knowing that my head coach was willing to vouch for my character.

I decided to just shake it off. I figured that McShay must have had me confused with someone else. But as you can probably imagine, Leigh Anne was not happy. She was so angry that someone would say something like that about one of her children without having met us. I think I might have had to calm her down a bit from going into full-on "mama bear mode."

When April 26 arrived, I was sitting in a room in Radio City Music Hall in New York City, waiting to hear my name. The Tuohys were all there, as was my big brother Marcus and Miss Sue. We were sitting in a room with a number of other players who were expected to go in the very first round. It was crazy to look around the room and see other big-name college football players like Matthew Stafford, Jason Smith, Eugene Monroe, Josh Freeman, Aaron Curry, Brian Cushing, and Michael Crabtree sitting with their families all trying to play it cool, even though I knew they were probably feeling every bit as on top of the world as I was.

One by one, their names were called. As they left the room for their photo ops, I was still sitting there. Finally, I was the last person left in the room and my heart started to sink. For a split second, I started to panic, thinking McShay's comments must have really spooked some coaches; or maybe they had believed that now that I had a family, my drive to prove something with my game was gone; or maybe they had read the book and incorrectly assumed I wasn't smart enough to learn the team's playbook.

But then I looked around and thought, "Michael, you are at the NFL draft. *You are at the NFL draft!* What were the odds of this just a few years ago? Who cares if you are the number one pick or the number one hundred pick—think of what you've accomplished and what you've gotten to be a part of!"

And just then, my phone rang. I was the number twenty-three overall pick, and I was moving to Baltimore.

I couldn't have been happier. I respected Coach John Harbaugh from his time with the Eagles before taking over as head coach for Baltimore and was thrilled at the idea of playing for him. I admired General Manager Ozzie Newsome, who was the first African American GM in NFL history and one of the most well-respected men in the league. And I couldn't help but smile a little that after all of my struggles in school, I was going to be playing for the only NFL team to be named for a work of literature. (The Ravens are named for the famous poem "The Raven," by Edgar Allan Poe, who lived and died in Baltimore.) Everything was coming together—it just all felt right. I was absolutely grinning in all of the pictures as I held up the purple and gold jersey while my family clapped proudly and brushed away tears.

After the big announcement and the photos, I had a lot of interviews. In one I said:

> *I'm just blessed to be here. I came from a neighbor-*
> *hood where no one makes it out—zero people make it*
> *out. Just to get invited to New York and be a part of all*

this type of stuff—it's amazing to me. I still can't believe it. . . .

One thing I always did was stay true to myself, and when you do that the people around you are going to stay the same. I've always been a good guy, a guy who cared, and nobody will look at me differently because I'm going to the NFL. Everybody still acts the same way—we don't change who we are.

They throw everything at you—a lot of things. But I took everything head-on. . . . You've got to make sure you take every small step when you're getting ready to go to the NFL because if you don't, that one small step can hurt you.

LATER, DURING THE SEASON, I had an interview with NBC commentator Bob Costas, and he pointed out how emotional I looked when Roger Goodell called my name that day at the draft. I agreed with Costas and told him, "I had had dreams about that moment coming years before—dreaming about having my name called and waiting for that moment. Because I know how hard I worked to get to that point—for so long—and had to go through so many things. It was just unbelievable and I couldn't wait for it."

But my dream wasn't just about getting there—it was about staying there. And I knew that day wasn't the end of a dream. It was just the start of my next stage in making it all come true.

CHAPTER SEVENTEEN

On Raven's Wings

People like to talk about "Cinderella stories," but Cinderella didn't get her happy ending without lifting a finger. She had to show up at the ball, be charming and smooth, and win over the prince. Of course she had help along the way, but ultimately it was up to her to make the fairy-tale ending happen.

When I was drafted in the first round by the Baltimore Ravens, I knew I had done the impossible. I hadn't just beat the odds; I had blown them out of the water. But the story isn't just about arriving at the pros. My goal had never been just to get the offer, or to sign the contract, or to get the paycheck. I wanted to *do* something, to know that I was working each day to do something with my potential, pushing myself to make sure that I was always giving my all. Making it to the pros wasn't the finish line for me. The world is full of people who got their big shot and then never did anything with it. I had come too far to just let being drafted be the end of my story.

I'D NEVER BEEN TO BALTIMORE. I'd never even been to Maryland. All I knew about the city was that it had some great sports history and some of the best seafood in the country. I didn't get to see much of it when I first arrived, either. I landed at Baltimore-Washington International Airport after it was already dark, and the Ravens representatives picked me up and drove me straight to the Castle, which is the team's training center and headquarters. It is a gorgeous building that really does look like a castle (both on the inside and outside—stone fireplaces, wooden halls, surrounded by acres of forest), but it also has a number of state-of-the-art workout facilities, including the NFL's biggest weight room. It blew me away. I was so excited to get to work, I wanted to start training right away!

But I wouldn't be able to jump into things immediately. I had to travel back and forth a few times to sign papers, meet people, and so on. And it took some doing to get me all moved in and settled in Baltimore before the start of training camp. I had to finish up at Ole Miss, pack up all my stuff, learn my way around my new city, find a place to live, and get the new place put together. Thankfully, my family put their skills to work right away to help me find a great home to rent, one that would be perfect as my Baltimore bachelor pad. Leigh Anne took care of all of the decorating and picking out furniture while I wrapped up everything I needed to back in Oxford and Memphis.

I ended up choosing a couple of my high school and college awards and framed jerseys to take up to Baltimore with me, but I didn't want to take them all. There's nothing like going back to visit your parents' house and seeing your old bedroom just how you left it. That's one of those little things that makes you feel at home again. But I wanted my new house to feel like a fun, relaxing place to be, too. I wanted it to be somewhere Collins and

S.J. would want to bring friends, and where my new teammates might want to come and hang out. So Leigh Anne helped me find a nice pool table (with Baltimore Ravens pool balls, of course), and some comfy couches that are set up in front of an enormous TV so that we have a great place to watch movies. You can't beat watching *The Godfather* on a big screen! The end result was a great house that isn't too fancy or extravagant, just a nice place for me to live and have friends over.

I wanted to be careful about losing my head over money. It's very tempting when you've spent most of your life with empty pockets to want to go crazy and buy everything you've ever dreamed of with your first big paycheck. But there are so many stories out there about people who become famous, start raking in huge amounts of cash—and then suddenly are bankrupt and don't seem to understand how it happened.

USA Today ran a story not too long ago with the headline "Michael Oher cautions NFL rookies on value of money, learning to say 'no.'" I was glad that they wanted to shine a positive light on my feelings about the subject because some people seemed confused that I would choose to rent instead of buy a house my first year, or that I don't wear flashy jewelry. I wanted to get to know the area so that I could take my time deciding where I wanted to live. That way, when I bought a house, it would be a smart investment and not just a rush job of trying to find the biggest, fanciest place I could just because I could afford it. And tons of jewelry—what's the point? You can't wear it when you're playing or practicing, and since that's my job, that's where I'll be spending most of my time. Besides, I'm not really into the party scene or nightclubs, which is the only place where wearing that stuff seems to make sense for an athlete.

Now, I'll admit that I do have a soft spot for cars. I think it's because growing up, I was always depending on the Memphis city bus system or walking, so having a nice car was something I could really appreciate. I have three cars, but one of them always stays in Memphis so I have something to drive when I'm home. (S.J. generously volunteered to look after it while I'm away.) One stays in Baltimore, and the other sometimes I will drive back and forth if I don't fly. But beyond that, if I find that I'm tempted to buy another car, especially if it is a really expensive luxury kind, I'll buy a remote control car instead and play with it around the house or in the driveway. I have a couple of them, so when friends come over we can have races and just act like big kids. It may not be quite as much fun as driving the real thing, but I think it's a lot more fun than to wake up one morning and realize that I burned through every last cent of my contract.

JUST LIKE WHEN I GRADUATED from high school, the summer after I graduated from college was no time to relax, either. Training camp started almost as soon as I moved to Maryland in July; it was intense but started out our season in an exciting way. Our first preseason game was August 13 against our neighborhood rival, the Washington Redskins. We won, 23 to 0. Our second preseason game was a 24 to 23 defeat of the New York Jets. The next two games were on the road, with a 17 to 13 win over the Carolina Panthers and a 20 to 3 win over the Atlanta Falcons. Even though they were just scrimmages that didn't count toward our final records, those four games really got us fired up for the season that lay ahead.

Our season opener was a home game versus the Kansas City Chiefs on September 13, 2009, and I was playing right tackle. Kickoff was at 1 p.m. at M&T Bank Stadium in Baltimore, and it was a gorgeous day—upper seventies and not overly sunny. Even in all of my years of imagining that moment when I would take the field as a professional athlete, I never dreamed of more perfect weather. And, of course, my family was in the stands, decked out in purple and gold and cheering like maniacs. I am sure I could pick out Leigh Anne's shout out of the 67,000 people there. With a 38 to 24 win to wrap things up, I couldn't stop grinning for at least the next twenty-four hours.

The next Sunday, we beat the San Diego Chargers on the road, 31 to 26, and moved to first place in the AFC North; then we were back at home for a 34 to 4 win over the Cleveland Browns. It was an amazing start to my rookie year.

I alternated between right tackle and left tackle the whole season and, thanks to an amazing team that pulled together and learned how to read one another as the games went on, I started to get more and more notice from the press. I was named a *Sports Illustrated* Mid-Season All-Pro, and in December I was named the NFL's rookie of the month. The Ravens made it to the playoffs with a Wild Card game against the New England Patriots at Foxborough Stadium on January 10. I was at right tackle and our 33 to 14 victory was made even better by the fact that we didn't allow a single sack the entire game.

We'd made it to the AFC-Divisional Round, one of the top eight teams of the season. Our next opponent was the Indianapolis Colts, who ended up making it all the way to the Super Bowl. Even though that game marked the end of our season, we had a pretty good record to look back on.

The Ravens averaged 24.4 points per game, which made us the NFL's ninth-best scoring team for 2009. In a league of thirty-two teams, that's pretty good. That year, 2009, was also a year that tied or set several franchise records: 391 points (which matched the 2003 total) and forty-seven touchdowns—twenty-two of which were rushing TDs. The team also racked up the franchise's second-highest number of yards at 5,619. Our line helped to protect quarterback Joe Flacco, who set six career-high records that season.

At the end of the season, having started all sixteen games, I was named to the All-Rookie team by the Pro Football Writers of America, and I was runner-up for the AP's NFL Offensive Rookie of the Year Award. It was a pretty amazing end to an amazing season.

But just because our season was over didn't mean that I could sit back and relax until training camp started up again in July. I know how many guys out there would love to take my job, and I know that the minute I stop pushing myself to get better, one of them will step up for the chance. I got my position because someone else lost his; that's the way the game works, and I always try to keep that in mind so I never take for granted the opportunities I've been given.

A lot of people want to know what it's like to be a celebrity, and I feel bad when the most honest answer I can give them is "I don't know." But it's the truth. I don't feel like a celebrity and I don't live like one. I try to stay grounded, live simply, pay cash for everything, and just focus on doing my job. I try not to get into the "celebrity" mind-set because then it becomes easy to think you can slack off just because you're a big name. It also means you've forgotten where you came from and the hard work and discipline that got you to this level of success. The minute you start thinking that your reputation is enough to carry you is the moment that you start to slip.

No matter where I am—if I'm in Maryland or Memphis or somewhere on vacation—I work out every day. When I'm home visiting my family, I always carve out a few days to drive down to Oxford for a couple of days of intense training at my old field and gym at Ole Miss. There are several former Rebels who do that, and the coaches have told us that it's a good thing for the younger players to see us there working out because some of the younger guys think that once you make it to the pros your work is done and it's just about collecting a paycheck. The truth is, once you make it to the pros, you have to work harder than ever.

That's really my goal—to be the hardest-working guy in the NFL. My conditioning coaches sometimes tease me because I am so stubborn about getting in my workouts. I never, ever miss a practice, never miss a training session. Some of my friends think it's funny that I'm working on flexibility with the goal of doing a full split. I know guys my size don't really seem like the bendy gymnast type, but I've heard that there are one or two tackles out there on other teams who can do the splits, so that's become one of my motivations: If they can do it, I should be able to, too. It's about always looking forward and making sure that you give your job all that you've got. If I lose my starting position, it had better be because there was someone out there with more talent, not because I just didn't push myself enough.

CHAPTER EIGHTEEN

The Blind Side

During my junior year of high school, while I was staying with the Tuohys but before I had moved in permanently, I met a childhood friend of Sean's named Michael Lewis. He was in town to talk to Sean for an article he was writing about their high school baseball coach for the *New York Times Magazine*, and he seemed to find me an interesting and surprising addition to their family.

Sean had picked Lewis up at the airport and brought him back to the house, where I was working on homework. I had become such a normal part of the Tuohys' lives by that point that I guess it didn't occur to them to mention that I was a part-time resident of the house. It seemed to really throw Lewis off to see me in the house with everyone acting as if it was the most natural thing in the world for a big kid from the ghetto to be working through algebra problems at the dining room table.

As for me, I didn't really give him another thought, since I was up to my ears in homework and sports practice. But apparently, curiosity about me and my story started eating away at

Lewis and would continue to bug him for about six months after he left.

In the meantime, Sean and Lewis struck up their friendship again and enjoyed laughing about their own teenage years growing up in New Orleans. Several times they ended up seeing each other while Sean was traveling on the road working as a commentator for the Memphis Grizzlies. They were hanging out together, in fact, when Sean got the call about the car accident I was in with S.J. my senior year of high school. The more Lewis was around our family, the more he started to wonder about my story. Lewis started asking Sean more questions about who I was, where I had come from, and why on earth I was living with them. Sean told him what he knew, but since I didn't like to talk too much about my past and I was still pretty quiet in general, there wasn't a whole lot that he could share except from the point that I'd started at Briarcrest.

Lewis talked to his wife about what he had learned from Sean, and his wife immediately felt it could be a great story and told him he should look into doing a piece for the magazine about me. He called his editor and pitched the story to him as a *Pygmalion* piece—a story about a young person from the poor side of town who has his life and opportunities turned around by learning what's necessary to succeed in mainstream society. Ironically, that very same play would end up being one of my favorite pieces of literature I was studying around that same time.

He began to do some digging to see what he could piece together about my past. In the meantime, my senior year started, my football really began to take off, and the college recruiting began to really crank up. The more Lewis tried to learn about me, the more he felt that there was too much of a story just for a magazine article. At the same time, he had begun to research the left tackle position for his next book, which, in his usual style, was going to be a study of how something seemingly minor changed the whole shape of the game. In this case, it was how Joe Theismann's career-ending injury when he was sacked by Lawrence Taylor in 1985 changed the nature of football. This led a lot of coaches to see the importance of the left tackle to protect right-handed quarterbacks (and right tackle for lefties). Basically, they need someone strong to protect their blind side, since they can't see how or when they are being charged. The position grew to be much more heavily scrutinized, trained for, and highly paid than before—and it could all be traced back to that one game.

Lewis quickly figured out that since I also played left tackle, he'd found a link for his story line: Something as small as enrolling in a private school or making a bond with the Tuohy family could change my life the way that one play on one night changed the game of football. He talked to his editor at the *Times* magazine again and they agreed that instead of the article they were planning to run, the magazine would instead get first dibs to run a chapter from the book that Lewis was going to write.

For the next year and a half or so, Lewis worked on his book, analyzing football rosters and team payrolls, as well as traveling to Memphis to talk to a lot of people who had known me when I was younger. A few times he would call Sean and Leigh Anne late at night to report his location, as he knew he was in some of the most dangerous neighborhoods in Memphis. I guess he figured if he got killed, they would know roughly his last location. He went by a lot of my old schools and old hangouts and tried to talk with anyone he could who had a connection to me, in an effort to piece together the details of my early life. Of course, by that point, I was getting to be a well-known college prospect and then a successful freshman at Ole Miss, so a lot of people suddenly were willing to step up and take credit for my success.

For a long time, though, I was pretty unaware of what Lewis was doing as he tried to get my story right for his book. He had talked to me about wanting to work me into a book he was working on, but that just sounded so crazy to me that I didn't give it a lot of thought and I didn't share much information with him. I mean, what was so interesting about me? Who would want to write a book about my life? What was there even to say that would fill up a newspaper column, let alone two hundred or more pages? Besides, I had tried to put a lot of stuff out of my mind in order to make it to where I was. At the time, I really couldn't see the point in pulling it all back up again. I just kind of figured he was some eccentric friend of Sean's and it would all blow over soon. Besides, I was starting college, so I had a lot more pressing things on my mind.

Eventually, I got the message that this Michael Lewis guy was actually planning to do something with my story. I had started hearing from people that he had talked to them about me—it seemed he had talked to everyone about me. So I decided to do two things that I thought were important: I googled his name and I gave him a call.

First of all, I wanted to learn more about him. I mean, it's only fair if he was trying to learn all about me, right? I typed in his name and read all about *Moneyball* and how he broke down the way that some baseball teams were able to build surprisingly good teams without having the highest payroll. What he said really made sense, and it occurred to me that maybe this guy knew a thing or two about sports after all. Then, when I saw that he had a number of other books published, too, I realized that he was definitely not just some weirdo with a tape recorder and a strange interest in the ghettos of Memphis.

When I called him from my dorm room at Ole Miss, I asked him the question he loves to share when discussing *The Blind Side*: "Are you the guy who keeps asking every other person in the world questions about me when you could just come and ask me?"

Yes, it turned out, he was that guy.

"Man, you're big time!" I laughed. And after that, we struck up a bit more of a conversation. He was just wrapping up his writing of the book, so the timing worked out well. After a couple of discussions, he felt he had the story he needed to help bring a human face to the position of left tackle.

I think we all sort of thought that that was the end of it all: The book was finished and probably would be a big hit with sports guys and people interested in strategy, and that was it. After all, no one gets that wrapped up in a football story, right? Obviously, we were wrong.

THE BOOK WAS RELEASED LATE in 2006. The *Times* chose to run as their exclusive scoop on the book a piece called "The Ballad of Big Mike," which was all about me and how I ended up where I was. The story was in the September 24, 2006, issue of the magazine, during the fall of my second year of college. To be honest, the book didn't really affect me much at first—initially I think it was mostly football fans who were reading it. It hadn't yet become a huge phenomenon.

Less than two years later, the movie rights were sold and Lewis was working on a screenplay with John Lee Hancock, who would go on to direct the movie. It turns out that football fans weren't the only people reading the book. Most people weren't excited about the ins and outs of the left and right tackle positions; they were connecting with the human side of the story.

Filming started in Atlanta in the spring of 2009 as I was finishing up my senior year of college and getting ready to graduate. I was way too busy focusing on the last of my classes to be too worried about any of that. I had heard that Sandra Bullock had signed on to play Leigh Anne, which seemed like good casting to me; Sandra seemed like she was strong enough to pull off the role in a way that would really help get Leigh Anne's personality across to people who didn't know her.

When the movie opened in New York in November, I couldn't go to the premiere. The Ravens were in the middle of their season and our next opponent was the Colts. There was no way I could take off time from getting ready for a game against one of our toughest opponents. The Tuohys all went, though. Leigh Anne was in a black evening gown; Collins wore a purple one. They both looked really beautiful from the pictures I saw. Sean and S.J. were both in suits, and S.J. wearing an Ole Miss tie, which I thought was pretty cool.

The film also had a debut in New Orleans the day after its New York premiere. That was a great choice, since Sandra cares a lot about that city. She bought a house there and has been helping support a lot of local students since Hurricane Katrina wiped everything out. Also, her little boy Louis was adopted from New Orleans, and she was quietly finishing up the last stages of that process as the movie was opening. Sean also grew up in New Orleans; his dad was a famous high school basketball coach with an amazing record and a great reputation as a character. So it made sense to celebrate the movie in a city that could really use some positive excitement. But again, I wasn't able to be there because of my work schedule and our upcoming game on Sunday.

As a matter of fact, I didn't end up seeing the movie until the season was over in early January. It had already been in the theaters for over a month by then, and I had several guys on other teams say, "Hey, Hollywood!" when we faced one another on the line. The funny thing was, they were mostly nice about the movie; several of them said they liked it a lot. For a bunch of guys who make a living trash-talking and tackling one another on the field, it was nice to know that they were happy for me.

When I finally went to watch it, I went with a couple of my teammates and just bought a ticket to the show like a normal person. I didn't tell anyone at the theater who I was or that the movie was about me. I just wanted to see it the way anyone else would.

My feelings afterward were mixed. First of all, I couldn't understand why so many people around me were sniffing and blowing their noses at the end. I wanted to stand up and say, "You realize that was a *happy* ending, right? I mean, I have a great life, a great family, and I am really thankful for all of the blessings I've been given. Things turned out really good for me—please don't cry."

But the other side of me had to deal with some wounded pride. I understand that there are certain things you have to do to make a story work as a movie; you may have to move some things around or play certain things up or down in order to help the audience buy into your characters and plot. I liked the movie as a movie, but in terms of it representing me, that's where I had a hard time loving it. I felt like it portrayed me as dumb instead of as a kid who had never had consistent academic instruction and ended up thriving once he got it. Quinton Aaron did a great job acting the part, but I could not figure out why the director chose to show me as someone who had to be taught the game of football. Whether it was S.J. moving around ketchup bottles or Leigh Anne explaining to me what blocking is about, I watched those scenes thinking, "No, that's not me at all! I've been studying—really studying—the game since I was a little kid!" That was my main hang-up with the film. I liked the book pretty well, but I knew more people were going to watch the movie than read the book and I really didn't want them to think I was someone who was so clueless about something I had always taken pride in being pretty smart about.

On the other hand, I'm glad the movie was a big enough hit that it could reach some kids who are in the same position I used to be in when I was in foster care. If my story in *The Blind Side* can help inspire them to find a way out of the ghetto, then it's all worth it to me.

CHAPTER NINETEEN

A Different Kind of Fan Mail

E very week, I get big boxes of fan mail that have been sent to the Ravens, to my parents' house, and to Ole Miss. Many are autograph requests or people wanting me to make an appearance at one event or another. I really appreciate the enthusiasm my fans show, but the volume is always way more than I can possibly handle, so I end up having to turn down a whole lot of requests.

There are some letters, though, that stand out to me. A handful of letters from just a typical week paints a pretty good picture of the kinds of people who have written to me because they've been touched by my story—by *our* story, really. What these letters tell me is that kids like me aren't the exception. There are a lot of us out there whose family life is unfortunately similar to mine, and whose struggles sound familiar. These letters come to me from Maryland, Kentucky, Mississippi, Oregon, California, Ohio—all over our country in every state and every community there are kids who are hurting. Some of these kids have had people step up to show them love; others are still waiting for someone to do that. All of them are desperate for a role model.

The stories I share below are all taken from just a couple of days' worth of fan mail. Some of the letters made me cheer, some made me smile, some made me want to cry. Some tell long stories and others are just a few lines on notebook paper. But all of them are an important look into a world many of us might never see otherwise.

I want to include them here not as a way to pat myself on the back for the positive words they give me, but because I want people to understand how big the need is, and how clearly kids like I was are hurting for someone to look up to and teach them how to make the right choices and reach their full potential in life.

"E" bravely shares her own experiences and struggles as she writes about being rejected by her mother while still in high school, losing an athletic scholarship in college, struggling with addictions, and being homeless until one woman stepped up to mentor her and a loving family stepped in to give her a home.

This happened in May of 2009 and I am still there. I am sober, I have a good place to live, I have a family, and I no longer feel lost, ashamed, abandoned, lonely, or hurt. I have a mom, dad, two younger brothers, and a dog. I am no longer on the run. I no longer have to be hungry every night. I no longer have to sleep on the ground, I have a bed, and I look forward to it every night. It is a warm, safe, comfortable, supportive, and loving, not abusive, environment. I finally have what I always wanted: a family that loves and cares about each other. Well, it took a long time to get here, and many

*times I felt like giving up along the way, but I made
it with the help of many people. I cannot say enough
good about these people. They opened up their house
to a stranger and allowed me to be a part of it, not an
outsider . . .*

*Your story let me know that I am not alone, and that
I am not the only kid who had a rough beginning—and
to never give up. Thank you for having the courage to
share your story on a much larger scale.*

In a completely different kind of letter, Molly writes to share
her story of a family who opened their hearts to a child who
needed a home:

*I am eleven years old and I was born in China.
My mom gave me away. I was adopted by two of the
greatest parents. My tale is simple and easy. You went
through so much more . . . You will always be one of
my greatest heroes and a wonderful role model. You
are amazing and I am always grateful for the people
that care about the homeless and poor. Keep changing
people's lives like you did with me.*

Betty describes her own experiences in reaching out:

*During the NFL draft, I was enthralled with the story
of your life. It mimics the story of my life. God decided
that in our family's lives should be a little abandoned
4½-year-old toddler of a different race. Today, she is
a wonderful, successful, beautiful woman. We are a*

*typical, very middle-class family that wanted to share
our blessings with someone that may not have what we
have . . .*

*Today, I volunteer at the high school that all my
children graduated from. I asked myself, why would I
volunteer EVERY DAY? Lo and behold, after one week,
I found the answer: a six foot four young man from the
streets of Cleveland, Ohio. I am just in the beginning
stages of getting to know him, teaching him, and guiding
him. Tomorrow we have our first outing. It is Martin
Luther King Day and I am taking [the student] and
his fellow basketball team members to the Cinemark
Movie Theater to see* The Blind Side. *We are taking
baby steps that started with a part-time tutor, clothes,
and food.*

*I am excited to begin my second version of the
"Michael Oher" story. May God continue to bless you!
You and your family are truly an inspiration!*

Lance and Becky share about the need they saw in their community and how it has helped their family grow in wonderful and unexpected ways:

*Your story has affected a seventeen-year-old young
man, Jyi. We met him over a year ago. He is a senior
football player at [our local high school]. He has had
many obstacles to endure during his life. He has lived in
different states and has been exposed to situations with
drugs, violence, and safety issues. He has had no option
but to grow up early and take on adult responsibilities
and financial stress. His childhood has thrown many*

*situations at him, which included . . . his family in and
out of the legal system, navigating through the school
system having dyslexia, and now his mother having a
cardiac condition that requires surgery. Because of this,
she has been unable to work and maintain their housing. As a result, he has come to live with my husband
and me and our three children.*

*When we were moving him in, my husband ham-
mered our wall just to get his bed in his room. This is
Jyi's first bed he has ever owned . . . My children think
of him as a brother. He goes to their games, helps them
with homework, and interacts with them like a big
brother. He shares his life experiences with my husband
and me. I am a social worker who works with at-risk
children and families. Even with this experience, I have
come even more to realize the importance of a mentor
and role model in a child's life. You have given him
the inspiration to keep moving forward and continue
to live the sport of football. He is making college site
visits and pursing a degree in criminal justice after
graduation . . .*

*Jyi has not only become a family member, he is now
mentoring some of my children's friends. He has shared
that he knows what it feels like to have someone give
you that attention and is now doing it for them. I feel
joy and peace when I hear him laugh. The sound of his
laughter is one I will never forget.*

*Despite all of his challenges, he has become a
delightful young man. He supports his mother; takes
her to all doctor appointments; helped her move—all
while attending school. She is in his life and has taught*

him how to be a strong, dependable, well-mannered
young man. She willingly shares the mistakes and
circumstances they encountered while he was growing
up, but continues to support him in his future plans.
I believe with all the challenges that arise, your story
enables him to make good choices and pursue his
dreams! . . . You are his favorite football player and
mentor . . . He considers himself the Michael Oher of
[our town]!

Other people, like Ms. Maureen Long of Mississippi Children's
Home Services, share encouragement about how my story has
helped children and the teachers who work with them to find hope
and promise in the future:

I am the principal of CARES School, which is a
private, state-accredited school that serves students
who have been identified as having special emotional
and behavioral challenges. Many of our students are in
the custody of the Department of Human Services and
have had many home placements. They are from six to
eighteen years of age. Currently, we have 102 students
enrolled. Your story has inspired me to continue to work
to help young people find their strengths and talents.

During the Christmas season our teachers went to see
The Blind Side. *We were so moved by your story that the*
teachers pooled their own resources to pay the admission
costs for our students to see the movie. The kids enjoyed
the movie, but seemed to think it was a "fairy tale." For
them, things like that don't happen in real life.

One of my goals is to help students identify their strengths and talents. In special schools, we spend most of our time working on students' weaknesses and needs. You are living proof that if someone takes time, resources, and the initiative, students can learn skills that directly lead to success in life!

. . . Again, I congratulate you on your success and the impact your story has had on the staff and students at CARES School!

Some of the most touching letters I receive are from groups like the YMCA/YWCA and the Boys and Girls Clubs. Ms. Charlene Hawkins, the Program Manager for Youth Services at the YWCA of Annapolis and Anne Arundel County, has shared with me the letters of several young people in her organization:

The reason why I am writing you is that we took our youth to see your movie, The Blind Side. *First, I want to thank you so much for allowing your life to be put on screen to inspire the youth of today. We really enjoyed the movie and the students had to write a letter to you to tell you how the movie inspired them. . . . I wanted you to see that your movie really blessed them.*

D. writes:

That movie inspired me because when I'm down, I never quit. And now I want to play the game of football . . . You inspired me to believe in myself. Thank you, Michael Oher. Thank you.

E. writes:

> *You had a tough childhood. That book and movie taught me not to hang with the wrong people even if they say "Do it."*

K. writes:

> *You have done so much in your life. I would like to be like you one day. Your movie taught me a lot of things, like school is important and family is a key role in life.*

L. writes:

> *Your life story has reached my heart as well as many others. I really look up and cherish you. Most famous people get blinded by the money and fame and forget where they come from, but you didn't. I can relate to your story. My mom was on drugs and my dad was abusive, but over the years things have gotten better and I learned to forgive them and let what happened in the past stay in the past and look forward to the future.*

Another wonderful set of letters arrived from Ms. Stacy Rulon at Sunrise Children's Services. She explains the organization's efforts:

> *I work in a program for teenage girls that are at risk and have behavior problems. We just watched the*

movie The Blind Side, *based on your life. It was very*
inspirational how you were able to overcome your past
and succeed in life. I think it showed our girls that it
is okay to give happiness a chance, that people can
be trusted and to give them a chance to care about
them . . . [Some girls from the program] wanted you to
know how they felt after watching the movie.

Unfortunately, because of the complications of getting permission from the parents or legal guardians of these children, I
won't be able to quote directly from what the students wrote. But
just to give you an idea of what these letters said, I will summa-
rize some of them.

One girl wrote to say that she had been in juvenile deten-
tion for about a year and didn't think she would even finish high
school. But the movie showed her that success isn't just for kids
from solid backgrounds and stable homes—it's something anyone
can pursue, and she is now inspired to go after real success, too.

Another girl talked about living on the streets after being
neglected by her mother. A friend's aunt took her in and did not
give up on her, even though she kept messing up. She is so grateful for that woman's concern and wants to know what advice I
could share about staying off the streets and out of trouble for
good. Another letter told a similar story, and how learning about
my life made her decide not to give up and motivated her to turn
her life around for her siblings to see and learn from.

There was a letter that talked about living in fear of facing life's problems. This young person had been taken from her
mother when she was twelve and felt like she had no way to stand
up for herself and make a better life. But she said that my story

made her believe that good grades and personal courage were possible for kids like her, and she thanked me for giving her that hope.

A teenager wrote to say that *The Blind Side* had been shown in the group home where she was living and it caused her attitude to change. She realized she couldn't just blame her circumstances and feel sorry for herself; in order to have a better chance at life she needed to change her own behavior and refuse to let other people's mistakes hold her back.

A different teenager told me how she had attempted suicide because she felt so alone, but her foster sister found her and begged her to stop, explaining that she was loved and wanted and not alone anymore. After watching the movie about my life, she realized for the first time that she wasn't the only kid who had felt those negative things. She saw that there was a hopeful future for kids like us if we just accepted the help and support of the people around us.

One girl explained how she and her older sister had been shuffled between relatives and then finally turned over to state custody. Her sister aged out of the system at eighteen, but this girl was still waiting and hoping for a family that might take her in as she finished school—because she is determined to graduate. My movie, she said, showed her that the only way to succeed is to believe that you can do it and that you are worth the effort.

Several kids wrote that they felt empowered by my story in a way they never had before—like I was giving a voice to all of them, making people aware of the kinds of challenges we face and showing the world that foster kids are strong and talented and want a future as much as every other child in the world.

———

IF ONE WEEK, chosen at random, can bring in this many letters, imagine the need out there. Imagine how many children are hurting and looking for help. Imagine how many wonderful families are stepping up to meet the needs of people like "E" and Molly and Jyi and others—and how many more are still needed.

While I may quibble with how I was depicted in the movie, I am truly grateful that my story has been such an inspiration. I hope it continues to inspire people to step up to help—to tutor, to coach, to become a foster parent. And I hope struggling kids are inspired to make choices that will empower them in life. My story is their story. Let's beat the odds together.

CHAPTER TWENTY

Breaking the Cycle

W henever someone finds out who I am, the two questions I'm always asked are: 1) Is the movie true? and 2) Who did you look up to as a kid? I talked about the first question back in chapter 18, but the second one isn't as easy to answer. The truth is, I didn't really have any one person I could look up to when I was younger—but I did have someone I could look to for how *not* to live my life: my mother.

It is so important for young people to have role models. In neighborhoods like the one I grew up in, it can be hard to find people who behave responsibly, hold down a solid job, support their families, and generally live lives they can be proud of. I really can't explain to someone who hasn't lived in poverty what it's like to struggle to find some kind of hope. I lived in a house where I had nobody to look up to, nobody going to work every day. Everyone in my neighborhood just seemed focused on trying to survive. And as well-meaning as they might be, many people who are trying to solve the problems of poverty haven't actually lived it, making it hard for them to really understand the daily struggles.

That's why I'm trying to get my message out there. In my case, and in the case of countless kids like me, what we see is the irresponsible choices our parents have made. And when that's what you're around day in and day out, when that's your world, you start to think that's the only way to live. I will always love my mother, but I never want to be like her. I decided back when I was still in school that I was not going to have her life. That's the challenge I want to extend to every kid who might be reading this book: Make the decision today to commit yourself to something better. It's going to take work and it's going to be tough at times, but you've already taken the first step by thinking about wanting something different. Patterns of thinking are the toughest habits to break, and I want to applaud you on your courage and strength to go for something more.

That's my goal with this chapter: to lay out the best advice I can offer to all the other Michael Ohers out there. Especially in my early years, I didn't have anyone modeling the life I wanted. I had to learn a lot of these lessons the hard way. I'm not trying to lift myself as a perfect role model—my life hasn't been perfect. But I am committed to stand up as a mentor for kids who are right where I was ten years ago.

Now that I have some time in the pros under my belt and the story of my life has suddenly become wildly interesting to everyone, I want to share the things that helped me to survive. It is my hope that this chapter will get photocopied and laid on many kids' pillows at night by loving foster parents, or slipped into backpacks by caring teachers who recognize a kid who is trying to fight against the odds. I want to see this chapter in the hands of every foster child in America so they will know how to work to make their dreams become a reality.

Just because the statistics say we're likely to fail doesn't mean that it has to be true for us.

THERE ARE A LOT OF THINGS you have to look out for. You have to keep an eye on your own conduct; you have to be careful about the friends you choose; you have to be on the lookout for mentors; you need to be ready to work hard; and you need to be smart about money. It may sound like a lot to juggle, but as we break it down, I think you'll see how it all comes back to your determination to make smart choices.

First of all, take a look at your family and think about what you can celebrate there. There may be a whole lot of negative stuff going on at home, but think about who you love there, and what you have learned in your life. Personally, I know that I have been so blessed in my life because, while some people pray for just one family to love, I have been given two. The Tuohys made me a part of their home, but my biological siblings are a part of my life as well.

My sisters and younger brothers never did end up coming back home from foster care; one of my little sisters, who was born while I was in middle school, was adopted by her father's family and enjoys a nice life with them now. But it is sad that our mother's choices ended up tearing our family apart so that I barely know some of my own family now.

Denise has her own apartment and job, and I am really proud her. I hadn't seen her since the day she was loaded into the car back in 1993, but we finally met up in 2009—it was great to see her after more than fifteen years. She is tall, like our mother and me, which for some reason made me really happy—I guess it's just knowing that we share something.

We older Oher boys have remained in pretty close contact with one another, and I've been able to enjoy having them as part of my life. One or another of my brothers always tried to make it to my football games in high school, and some of them even made it to a couple of my college games. Marcus, as I mentioned, was with me on draft day, which was really special, too.

My junior year of college, Deljuan was killed when the car he was riding in with Marcus and Rico hit a pole. That was really tough to go through; I left classes for a few days to go home for the funeral and cry together as a family. It was so hard to lose someone who had been such a huge part of my life. I always kind of thought of my big brothers as one big unit that no one could hurt or break up, even if we were living in different places. Of course, as kids we had to fend for ourselves a lot, but their love was always important to me, and even now I am proud of how we tried to stick together. Now Carlos is a dad and Marcus, too—he's married and has a little house in Memphis.

When I got my first paycheck from the Ravens, I gave each of my brothers a little bit of money—just enough to buy a reliable used car to get them to and from work. I wanted them to know that it was important to me that they have a way of supporting themselves. I also took them shopping to get some work clothes, but my mother got ahold of it all and sold whatever she could as soon as I was out of town.

She called me later and left a message on my voice mail calling me some really terrible names for taking them shopping and not her. I must have listened to that message a hundred times, and each listen hurt as much as the first one. When I tried to talk to her about it, she yelled at me, "You've got to answer to God."

"No, *you've* got to answer to God," I finally said to her. "I'm just trying to do right by my brothers."

I will always love my family—my siblings and my mother—and we have been through a whole lot together. But that doesn't mean that I need to keep negative people in my life. My biological mother has shown me time and again through her poor decisions that she values certain things more than she values her relationship with her children. I've tried to put her in rehab, I've tried to help her however I could, but I have finally realized the sad truth—that she and I really don't have a relationship anymore. When I was sixteen, she started back into her old ways after being clean for a couple of years. I've talked to her since then, but I haven't had a real *conversation* with her. We have nothing to talk about. The choices we have made are so different that it feels like we have nothing at all in common, and when I try to connect with her, she only acts resentful.

I just have to remember the good times—the way she was when she was off drugs and working—and decide for my own life what kind of parent I am going to be once I get married and start a family. All she did was give birth to us. She was never really a mother, not in any reliable way. I know that I am not going to do anything to bring children into this world until I can provide a good life for them with a solid family, and I'm going to make sure that I am grateful for them. I'm going to be a great father, do all the right things, and make sure I'm there for them. My mother's failures do not have to be mine.

You need to make that same decision. If a family member is abusive or neglectful, you can always be grateful that person gave you life or shares your genes, but you also have the power to recognize that their life is not your life and their decisions do not have to be yours. It may be that you are able to separate yourself from that person, painful as it might feel, and refuse to allow their poisonous way of acting to influence your life anymore. Of course, it could be that you are not able to physically remove yourself from the situation. In that case, then, you just have to decide in your own mind who you are, what you want, and what it is going to take for you to get there. Keep that in the front of your mind at all times and never let that other person knock down your dreams or pull you off-course.

The same is true when it comes to choosing your friends. It can be really tough to find good people to hang around with, and it can be lonely sometimes. It's impossible to stress how important it is that you choose the right friends, no matter who you are. It doesn't matter if you're a poor kid in the projects or someone in foster care bouncing around to different neighborhoods or a rich kid in a private school. The people you choose to hang out with are going to have a huge impact on the choices you make and the person you end up becoming. If you hang around people who are always negative, you're going to start acting that way, too, because it will just seem normal. If you spend all your time with people who get into trouble, you're going to end up getting into trouble, too. You have to keep your eyes open for the right kinds of friends if you want to go against the trends around you.

I was lucky enough to find Craig, and I am so glad that I did because I know his influence helped keep me out of serious trouble. I try to include him whenever I hang out with my brothers because he is just like a brother to me. I'm so proud of him for having a steady job and keeping such a clean life—no drugs, arrests, or any of that mess. He's still a good guy and I love him for it.

Jamarca, who was such a good friend to me while we were in college together, is another guy who has his head on straight. We looked out for each other during college and we still stay close now that we're both in the pros. He plays for the Vikings, but when he's not in Minnesota, we rent a place together in Oxford to be near the Ole Miss campus for workouts. He's someone I know I can trust to not pull me into trouble or try to get me involved in the wrong things.

It blows my mind when I look around and see those professional athletes who keep hanging around thugs and hustlers and other people who are just plain bad news. When the people in the entourage cause trouble, the athlete almost always gets into trouble, too. Look at Michael Vick. He is actually a nice guy and a talented player; but after he made it big, he kept hanging around with troublemakers from his old neighborhood, and that was how he ended up involved in the dog fighting ring that landed him in prison.

The friends you choose can make all the difference as to where you end up. If all of your friends cut school, don't do any work, hang out with thugs, or are involved in bad activities, chances are good that you'll end up doing the same thing. It's crazy to think you can be surrounded by all that and not be tempted to join in. If you want to get out of the ghetto, you can't keep living like the ghetto.

There is sometimes a sense of "They knew me when, so I owe them. Otherwise, I'm a sell-out and disloyal." I appreciate the idea of not forgetting where you came from, but a true friend wants you to succeed for who you are and not for what you can give them. In my senior yearbook at Briarcrest, each of us was supposed to include a quote as our parting thought at graduation. I adapted a line from a rap song and from the movie *Hoop Dreams*: "People ask me if I ever reach the top will I forget about them? So I ask people if I don't reach the top will y'all forget about me?" It's unfortunate, but things change when you start succeeding, and I wanted to know who was going to stick with me even if I didn't make it.

While you are coping with any negative influences in your family or from your friends, you should always be keeping your eyes open for positive influences. Try to find those mentors wherever you can, because they will become a new kind of family for you. In my case, they literally became family when the Tuohys took an interest in my life and helped me grow into everything I could be. But there were other mentors, too, who I've talked about in this book. They all helped me, in their own way, to see that there was something more than the way of life I knew, and they each gave me a little boost toward reaching it. It is so important to find someone who can show you how to make good life choices and how to live responsibly. That kind of wisdom is a gift whose value can't be measured.

I've been very blessed to have some great mentors and friends in my life. I know that they all made a difference—some big and some small—but every positive thing had an impact and helped get me to a place where I was able to achieve my potential. People like Ms. Spivey and Velma were mentors to me, even though I didn't realize it at the time. They had my best interests at heart and were trying to help me find a better path than the one I was on. Tony and Coach Johnson, Steve and Craig, were all that kind of mentor for me, too. Maybe it sounds strange to have mentors who were kids, but I admired the dedication and character Steve and Craig had, and I know that having them around helped keep me out of some of the more serious trouble I could have found.

The role of a mentor is so important, but it's not an easy one for either party involved. It can be tough for an adult to wade through all of the trust issues, bad behavior, and attitude problems that a kid has picked up because they were never taught any different. For a kid, it can be hard to accept that someone might actually have your best interests at heart—that you can trust them to be true to their word and to really care about you. It can be a challenge not to be closed off or to keep your head down, or worse, to put on an act of being cocky and full of yourself.

No matter what is going on around you that you can't control, your attitude is the one thing that you *can* control. Think about how much better you are than your circumstances. Just by being able to recognize that fact, you're already light-years ahead of people who let other people's mistakes control them.

Another challenge to consider in looking for role models is one I personally struggled with—the thought that no one could possibly care about a kid like me enough to really want to get involved. It was hard for me to believe that anyone had that much love, to believe there's that much love out there anywhere in the world. Of course there are people out there who have love like that, but coming where I come from, you're not going to meet many of those people.

If I hadn't ended up at Briarcrest or been taken in by the Tuohys, I would have had to take a different route, of course. Maybe I'd have gone the junior college route to a football career. Maybe I wouldn't have had a football career at all. I might have tried to do it and failed. In fact, if I wasn't in the NFL, I wouldn't have one job—I'd have two. As I like to joke with Sean, I might be working at a Taco Bell instead—and I don't mean like how he works at Taco Bell by owning a bunch of them. I mean, I'd be inside as the guy taking your order. But you know what? That would have been all right, too. Because it is a respectable job that doesn't depend on a welfare check, and doesn't involve breaking the law or hurting people.

That's the most important lesson I want people to take from this book: You don't have to get adopted by a rich family to make it. You don't have to get adopted by anyone at all. You just have to have it set in your brain that you are going to make a better life for yourself and you have to be committed to making that happen.

You can't sit around and wait for a loving family to show up and help you out because, unfortunately, that might never come. You have to be committed to chasing your dream yourself, and if someone steps up and helps you along the way, that's awesome. But if not, it's still up to you what you do with your life. You can blame circumstances or whatever you want to, but it's your life. You've got to be the one who is determined to make it succeed. No one else can do that for you.

If you're good at writing, you have to commit to keep growing. Read good books, magazines, or newspapers so that you can learn what to do to keep improving. If you're good at art, keep practicing it so that you can get new skills and learn new techniques that will open you up to new opportunities. If you are a talented musician, spend your spare time practicing or join a music club after school at the YMCA or Boys and Girls Club.

Your talents are a gift. Are you just going to drop them, hoping that someone will give you your dream job and a fat salary just for being you? Or are you going to take responsibility for what you've got and really push yourself to do something great with those gifts? You have to believe in yourself enough to know that you've got talent and that you are worth the investment of time and effort. God valued you enough to give you those abilities. Value yourself enough to grow those talents to become great.

SUCCESS IS DETERMINED by a lot more than what is in your bank account, but you do need to learn how to make good decisions about your money once you start earning it. There are a lot of very famous people who have earned a ton of money but don't understand basic things like self-control and discipline. As I mentioned in chapter 17, it amazes me how some pro athletes can sign multimillion-dollar contracts and be broke in six months, but it happens all the time.

Many churches and civic groups offer courses on learning how to make a budget and manage income. I would encourage anyone, but especially young people, to sign up for one. Believe me, I still think, "Wow! This is crazy!" every time I check my bank statement. It's really hard to get used to seeing a lot of zeros when you're used to just seeing one. It's exciting and fun to think you can provide for yourself with your own paycheck, but, unfortunately, a lot of other people think it's exciting and fun for you to provide for *them* out of your paycheck, too.

I have people hitting me up for money all the time. Sometimes they are people I don't know—a lot of inventors who want someone to invest in their product; a lot of wannabe rappers who want someone to pay for them to put out a record. Those are usually pretty easy to say no to. Sometimes the requests come from people I do know—people from back home in the old neighborhood who think I owe them; members of my father's family who I've never spoken two words to before. Those can be a bit harder to turn down.

I tell you those things because you've got to be prepared that with even the smallest amount of success, there are going to be people who feel like you should be paying their way. You don't have to be famous to get hit up for money—there are a lot of people out there who think they are entitled to anything you've earned just because you used to be neighbors or are family. And even if you have signed a big contract, once you pay taxes on a million dollars, there isn't nearly as much left over as most people think there is.

It's wonderful to help out people in need, or to donate to charities or causes that you believe in. I think that is a great thing and I would encourage everyone to do that. But you also have to have limits; you have to know when enough is enough. There is not enough money in the world to give everyone what they want. What you need to be aware of is how you handle the tough job of saying no when people ask you and you can't meet the need or don't think it's where you want your money to go. Don't let anyone guilt you into thinking your success obligates you to them; that's one of the quickest ways to get sucked back into poverty.

Remember the story of the Little Red Hen? She grew the grain and harvested it and baked it into the bread and no one wanted to do any of that work along with her . . . but they all wanted a piece of the bread when she took it out of the oven. If you do the work to get yourself a job, to put yourself through school, to work hard for good grades, to go without in order to save money and make smart spending choices—whatever it is that you need to do to achieve your dream—don't let anyone else claim your success as their own. There may be people who cheer you on along the way, and you should be sure to acknowledge and thank them, but don't let anyone try to guilt you out of what you've earned.

IT'S ALSO IMPORTANT to really study how to behave properly in different situations. Like I said in chapter 13, you need to be aware of different ways of acting that are appropriate for different situations. It doesn't mean that you're putting on airs or not being true to yourself if you act differently in one type of situation than another; it means that you have the discernment to know what is acceptable for each occasion. The same is true with how you dress. Your clothes don't have to be expensive, they just have to be neat in appearance and fitting for where you are.

Think about it: If you want a job in an office, you can't walk into the interview in jeans and an untucked T-shirt, or a really short skirt and low-cut blouse, laughing loudly on your cell phone and using curse words—right? That isn't presenting yourself in the right kind of way for that situation.

If you want to be a part of the professional world, you have to know how to act, dress, talk, and carry yourself. Look around at the people in the field you want to pursue, and make notes about how they come off. How does a businessperson act? How does a lawyer dress? How does a teacher speak? Study their behavior and even ask questions. By figuring out what it takes to present yourself in a certain kind of way, you can take huge steps in going after the kind of life you want. That doesn't mean you have to stop being who you are; it just means that you understand the difference between casual situations and professional ones. Those are some of the personal choices that will help set you apart from the way of living you want to escape.

Because, in the end, it all comes down to your choices. There is an old expression that life is 10 percent what happens to you and 90 percent what you make of it. It's true that we can't help the circumstances we're born into and some of us start out in a much tougher place than other people. But just because we started there doesn't mean we have to end there.

And there is just one more thing I want to encourage young people to think about. Don't ever allow yourself to feel trapped by your choices. Take a look at yourself. You are a unique person created for a specific purpose. Your gifts matter. Your story matters. Your dreams matter. You matter. The decisions you make this year, this month, this week, this day, this hour—they all matter, too. Each good choice you make is an investment in your future. You can get a better life. If you are willing to roll up your sleeves and work for it, then you certainly deserve it.

We are all in this together. I'm pledging my support to be the best role model I can be through the appearances and speeches I make for the various foster care support groups I work with, as well as with my lifestyle and the choices I make. I hope each child reading this book will pledge to value their life enough to commit to making it no matter what; and that every adult will pledge to find a way—any way—to give back.

If we all believe we can achieve something great, then I know that together, we can beat the odds, one life at a time.

CHAPTER TWENTY-ONE

Ways to Get Involved

f you are a concerned adult who would like to get involved but aren't sure where to start, there are a lot of places you can contact. The organizations I talk about here are not a complete list of all those out there. This chapter is really just a starting point to let people know the types of groups and opportunities available.

The most obvious place to start is to contact the guidance counselor at any local school. A counselor will be able to let you know if there are children in the school who have specific needs, like shoes or clothes. Or the school may have a mentoring program. Every school system has different rules and needs, but the guidance office is a great place to get started.

Just judging from some of the organizations that people have written me from, there are a lot of great groups out there that are making a difference in kids' lives.

There is probably a **YMCA** or **YWCA** in a community near you, and they are always offering classes and sports activities for kids who want positive ways to fill their time and develop their skills. These centers are often looking for volunteers to help coach, teach, or tutor, and can be a really good place to start making connections with individual kids.

Another good option for getting involved is the **Boys and Girls Club**. With more than four thousand clubs around the country, plus military bases, Puerto Rico, and the U.S. Virgin Islands, this is one of the biggest youth organizations in the world; and since there are clubs in every state, there is almost certainly one in a community near you. These are great places for children to find all kinds of help that they need, from academic support to after-school activities. And there is always a need for volunteers to help support the different programs offered.

Big Brothers Big Sisters is also a great mentoring program that offers one-on-one interaction for kids who are looking for positive role models and adults who want to have a direct impact on someone's life. There are programs in all fifty states and twelve countries internationally, so there are a lot of places and ways to make a difference.

Study Buddy is a national program that provides homework help online for kids who need some extra tutoring in math and science. It is part of the National Science & Technology Education Partnership, and its goal is to make "economics and geography no longer a bar to success in math. The linking of high school student tutors, one-on-one and online, with struggling middle and high school math students creates a community of role models for the struggling students in an unintimidating and exciting environment."

I strongly recommend you pick up the phone and call your local branch of any one of these organizations.

THERE ARE ALSO A NUMBER OF PROGRAMS that are dedicated specifically to children who have been placed in protective custody or are in foster care.

One group for which I've done some speaking is the **Treehouse** organization in Seattle, Washington. Their slogan is "Giving foster kids a childhood and a future," and their entire purpose is to help kids and families who are a part of the system. They have six different branches that offer different kinds of support:

- The Wearhouse, a free store where kids can get shoes, school supplies, books, and toys
- Little Wishes, which takes care of life expenses like drivers' education or classes to develop a certain skill
- Summer Camp, which gives kids a camp vacation to make new friends and just have a good time being kids
- Tutoring, which provides academic support for kids to teach them how to learn, study, and apply themselves
- Educational Advocacy, a statewide effort to give foster kids equal access to a stable education
- College and Career Planning, which lets older students explore different options for the future, either in terms of a career or working toward a college degree

Treehouse is an incredible group that helps hundreds of kids each year. But in order to do what they do, they have to have volunteers who not only donate funds but also give their time to do things like organize donations to the Wearhouse, or give music or dance lessons for free or at a reduced cost. I mentioned this group because I have worked with them in the past and I'm familiar with the great work that they do, but there are lots of organizations like Treehouse in other cities. If you aren't in the Seattle area, call around to see what programs might be doing similar work near where you live.

Aspiranet is an organization in California that works to help foster children and families feel supported. They also work to help children who are eligible for adoption find forever families. **House of New Hope**, a private Christian non-profit group does similar work in Ohio. **Jewish Child and Family Services**, based in Chicago, has programs in place to meet the huge need in that city. **CEDARS**, a Nebraska-based organization, has several programs, including one that helps kids who try to run away. The **Searcy Children's Home** in Arkansas specializes in helping siblings stay together in foster care.

In New York, **Little Flower Children and Family Services** specializes in helping abused and neglected children to help match them with strong, supportive families. They work with at-risk teens, too, to help straighten out their lives before they get into trouble and land in state custody. Their work also reaches out to disabled adults and seniors. Also in the northeast is **Casey Family Services**. They work in Connecticut, Maine, Maryland, Massachusetts, New Hampshire, Rhode Island, and Vermont, and provide "Foster care and adoption; family advocacy, preservation, and reunification; adoption support and other post-permanency services; [and] community-based family strengthening and resource centers." The **Martin Pollak Project** is an organization in Baltimore that offers help with placement and support for foster kids and children who have recently aged out of the system; the **Center for Family Services** offers resources and support for foster parents in the city, too. The **Tennessee Foster and Adoptive Care Association** is one that does the same kind of work in my own home state, and **Monroe Harding, Inc.** in Nashville offers a lot of different care options, too.

Youth Villages provides family structure and support for children in foster care across the southeast in Alabama, Arkansas, Florida, Georgia, Mississippi, North Carolina, Tennessee, and Texas, and also in the northeast in Massachusetts, New Hampshire, and Washington, D.C. A great feature about this organization is that it offers help to people up to twenty-two years old. So instead of just telling a kid "Good luck—you're on your own now!" when they age out of the system at eighteen, it gives older kids in the foster care system a transition period to look forward to as they finish high school and look to start a trade school, college, or full-time work.

There are also a number of group homes and teen ranches all over the country. The **Florida Baptist Children's Homes** have fourteen locations around the state to provide group home care for children in state custody. **Methodist Home for Children** is just one organization that places, supports, and advocates for foster children around the state of North Carolina. **Sunrise Children's Services** operates in Kentucky and has a lot of different programs and locations around the state, from group homes to family support.

There are also the **Cal Farley's Boys Ranch** (outside Amarillo, Texas) and **Cal Farley's Girlstown, U.S.A.** (outside Lubbock, Texas), which offer group home options and have strong records of success. The affiliated **Family Resource Centers** in Amarillo, Austin, Dallas/Fort Worth, Houston, and San Antonio help families that are struggling to stay together and provide stable environments for their children, and support for the children who are trying to make it through school and become contributing members of society.

In Missouri there are at least a half dozen places like **Whetstone Boys Ranch** in West Plains, which is a new organization doing a lot of great work already; **Lives Under Construction Boys Ranch** in Lampe, which works with boys ages seven to twenty-one; and **Coyote Hill Children's Home** in Harrisburg, which supports children from a lot of different types of family backgrounds. **Drumm Farm** in Independence specializes in caring for foster children, as well; Brodie Croyle, quarterback for the Kansas City Chiefs, does work with them. He grew up around that kind of environment because his father, John Croyle, established the **Big Oak Boys Ranch** and **Big Oak Girls Ranch** in his home state of Alabama.

I know of a number of other really good ranches/group home environments like these in just about every state—some are state-run, some are private, some are religious. It's worth doing a little research to find one that is a good match for your own interests so that you can feel good about your involvement. I should also add that places like these are usually happy to take all kinds of donations, sometimes even including gifts of older-model cars to help teach the young men auto repair. You get a tax write-off and the boys get a chance to learn responsibility and job skills.

In addition to Brodie Croyle, there are other athletes who are involved with helping foster kids, too. Myron Rolle, former Florida State All-American and Rhodes Scholar, runs a camp in the summer called the **Myron Rolle Wellness and Leadership Academy.** More than one hundred foster kids get the chance to hear motivational speakers, learn about physical fitness and nutrition, and most important, work on the confidence and skills to become good leaders. **Athletes for Charity** is an entire organization devoted to helping pro sports figures get involved in supporting and encouraging foster kids.

Some people have come up with creative ways to raise support and awareness. In August 2010, the singer Jimmy Wayne, who grew up in foster care himself, walked 1,700 miles from Nashville to Phoenix. His trip halfway across America was part of his **Meet Me Halfway** project, which aims to bring attention to older children in foster care who are aging out of the system.

Bethany Christian Services is a nationwide organization that helps match foster children with adoptive families and helps adults looking to become foster parents learn valuable skills to reach the children put in their care. The **Dave Thomas Foundation for Adoption** has as their slogan "Finding Forever Families for Children in Foster Care." Started by Dave Thomas, the founder of Wendy's, they are one of the county's biggest promoters of foster care awareness and adoption-support organizations. And **AdoptUsKids** has helped more than 13,500 foster children around the United States find permanent adoptive families.

Of course, don't forget to keep your eyes open for the need right in front of your face. Leigh Anne and Sean call this "popcorn giving," meaning you take care of the needs that pop up right in front of you. You don't need to have a school or a formal program to get involved. The Tuohys and other families at Briarcrest didn't. They didn't go looking for a needy kid to help; they didn't just close their eyes when one crossed their path. They saw a need and they each met it however they could.

Like I said, this is just a short list that barely scrapes the surface of all the great programs out there. I feel bad that I can't mention them all, but I hope this will at least give you some ideas of places where you can find help or offer help.

The problem of abused, neglected, and at-risk children isn't just a challenge in the inner city or in rural communities. It's everywhere. It's in every neighborhood and every school. If you grew up with a loving and supportive family, think about what they gave you. Was there someone there who cheered you on and challenged you to do better? Was there someone who guided you toward good decisions and away from bad ones? Now imagine that was taken away from you. Try to imagine what your life would have been like to have none of that support there. What would you have done? Would you be enjoying the same life you have today?

This is a problem we should all care about. These kids are the next generation, for better or for worse. Let's all do what we can to give them the best shot possible at success. Think of the difference you could make—that you may already be making—just by looking around you.

ACKNOWLEDGMENTS

Michael has experienced more in his twenty-four years than many people experience in an entire lifetime, and in order to really gain a fuller sense of all he has seen and lived we needed the help of many, many other people, ranging from family and friends to foster parents, former teachers, and DCS workers. Without their assistance we could have never helped Michael put together as complete a picture of his early life.

Ms. Bobbie Spivey is someone we cannot thank enough, not only for the time she gave us and the details she provided, but for the blood, sweat, and tears she dedicated to the Oher family and many others just like them for well over twenty years. Being a social worker is often a thankless job, but the dedication men and women in the field show is tremendous, important, and life changing. Thank you for all that you did and continue to do for the abused, neglected, and troubled children across the country.

Special thanks must be extended to Rob Johnson and Stacy Miller at the Tennessee Department of Children's Services. Together with the staff there, they dedicated days searching for

Michael's records—even in the midst of the devastating Nashville floods that were impacting their city—and spent hours with us on the phone, explaining the breakdown of the system in the 1990 and how to help Michael find alternative sources of information about his past, and advising us on the delicate legal restrictions involved. Thank you, too, to Nancy Clark who put us in touch with the right people; to Zach Farrar, for his help with navigating the juvenile court system in Tennessee; and to the Shelby County Juvenile Court, for the records and documents they were able to provide.

Thank you to Velma Jones, for meeting with us and supplying us with many details about Michael's time under her care, and to Ms. Verlene Logan, for talking to us about having Michael in her fourth-grade class. The memories you shared were fascinating and informative.

Michael's family, especially Marcus, was invaluable, not only for the stories they shared, but also for helping to take us around to visit all the old neighborhoods. Craig Vail was a great help in that regard, too; thank you for being such a loyal friend and a strong support. Steve Henderson, you are such a hard worker and we appreciate you taking the time out of your work schedule and celebration upon having just graduated from Ole Miss to share with us some of your memories of Michael. Big Tony Henderson, thank you for making time for us, too, and for your interest and concern for Michael even as you were focusing on raising your own sons to be successful men.

To Sean, Leigh Anne, Collins, and S.J. Tuohy, thank you for all of your time and help with both stories and photos for this book. You always give us something to laugh about, and your family has certainly made an impact on many, many lives.

Of course, this story wouldn't have caught America's attention if not for the amazing writing of one of this country's great writers, Michael Lewis, who penned the book *The Blind Side*. His book was spun into an even more amazing movie that was viewed by millions.

To Jimmy Sexton, John Haun, Heather Mundy, and everyone at Athletic Resource Management: Your help with coordinating all of the different pieces for this book was absolutely essential, and we are sincerely grateful for all of the energy, assistance, and support you provided in helping us to complete this journey into Michael's past, as well as looking ahead to a very bright and promising future.

To Megan Newman and Miriam Rich at Penguin: Thank you for your tireless work editing this manuscript, helping us craft it into something that will have the maximum impact and truly reach people with the heart of Michael's life and message. The great work of literary agent Scott Waxman made sure this story was told by the best possible publishing house.

Tiffany Yecke Brooks, who has been a wonderful partner during many writing projects, threw her heart and soul into this one. Her love of great stories and ability to help tell them made this come together.

The staff of the Baltimore Ravens was essential in helping us with fan mail, as well as allowing Michael the time he needed to work on this project. The Ole Miss staff was very accommodating in allowing us to work even while Michael trained. And the administration and teachers at Briarcrest Christian School were welcoming, warm, and helpful as we toured the grounds and conducted interviews. We are so grateful for the outpouring of support and encouragement that everyone at these schools provided for Michael.

And, finally, special thanks go out to the countless fans who cheer Michael on every week, especially to the ones who take the time to write to him, sharing their own stories, and to those who allowed us to print their letters. You are so brave and so strong. You matter. Thank you for trusting Michael enough to share such personal testimonies. Your letters mean the world to him, and they are the reason he strives each day to continue to succeed—to show you that dreams can come true. To the young men and women in the foster care system and to those wonderful individuals and organizations that work with them every day, this is for you.